*The Heritage of Literature Series*

SECTION B NO. 77

# THEATRE TODAY

*The Heritage of Literature Series*
*General Editor: E. W. Parker, M.C.*

This series incorporates titles under the following headings:
Travel and Adventure, Animal Stories, Fiction, Modern Classics,
Short Stories, Prose Writing, Drama, Myths and Legends, Poetry.

Each title in the series falls into one of three main sections:
Section A, without notes
Section B, with introduction and notes suitable for intensive
study
Section J, for younger readers

Other titles in the Drama Section of the series include:

A complete list of the series is available on request.

# THEATRE TODAY

*Edited by*
DAVID THOMPSON

LONGMANS

LONGMANS, GREEN AND CO LTD
48 Grosvenor Street, London W1
*Associated companies, branches and representatives
throughout the world*

PRINTED IN GREAT BRITAIN BY
NORTHUMBERLAND PRESS LIMITED
GATESHEAD ON TYNE

# ACKNOWLEDGEMENTS

We are grateful to the following for permission to include copyright material:

ACTAC (Theatrical and Cinematic) Ltd. for *Then* by David Campton, and *The Black and White* and *The Last to Go* by Harold Pinter; John Calder Ltd. and Grove Press, Inc. for *The New Tenant* by Eugene Ionesco; Jonathan Cape Ltd. and Howard McCann Inc. for *The Sandbox* by Edward Albee; the author for *The Interview* by J. P. Donleavy; the author and the author's agents Curtis Brown Ltd. for *It Should Happen to a Dog* by Wolf Mankowitz; the author and Macmillan & Co. Ltd. for *Hall of Healing* from *Collected Plays, Volume III,* by Sean O'Casey; the Public Trustee and The Society of Authors for *Passion, Poison and Petrifaction* by George Bernard Shaw; the author and the author's agents Laurence Pollinger Ltd. for *The Oyster and the Pearl* by William Saroyan; New Directions for " Between Walls " by William Carlos Williams from *Collected Earlier Poems* published by Macgibbon and Kee Ltd.

All applications for performance rights in these plays should be addressed to the following:

ACTAC Ltd. of 16 Cadogan Lane, London S.W.1 for *Then* by David Campton and *The Last to Go* by Harold Pinter; Jonathan Cape Ltd. of 30 Bedford Square, London W.C.1 for *The Sandbox* by Edward Albee; Rosica Colin of 4 Hereford Square, London S.W.7 for *The New Tenant* by Eugene Ionesco; the author c/o Penguin Books Ltd. of Harmondsworth, Middlesex, for *The Interview* by J. P. Donleavy; Samuel French Ltd. of 26 Southampton Street, London W.C.2 for *The Black and White* by Harold Pinter; The League of Dramatists of 84 Drayton Gardens, London S.W.10 for *Hall of Healing* by Sean O'Casey; the author c/o Curtis Brown Ltd. of 13 King Street, London W.C.2 for repertory rights and Evans Brothers of Montagu House, Russell Square, London W.C.1 for amateur rights in *It Should Happen to a Dog* by Wolf Mankowitz; the author c/o Laurence Pollinger Ltd. of 18 Maddox Street, London W.1 for *The Oyster and the Pearl* by William Saroyan; The Society of Authors of 84 Drayton Gardens, London S.W.10 for *Passion, Poison and Petrifaction* by George Bernard Shaw.

# Contents

# INTRODUCTION

The theatre, like all the arts, has its experimental or *avant-garde* side, and all experiment in the arts, precisely because it is trying to express something new, is liable at first to be misunderstood or not understood at all. But the theatre is essentially a public art, and it cannot really afford to be much misunderstood. If it doesn't interest or entertain large numbers of people, it goes out of business.

One of the most instructive things about the theatre in recent years has been the way in which a certain 'experimental' type of play, which would formerly have been almost impossible to write, let alone put on publicly before a paying audience, has come to be widely accepted, appreciated, and even, in one or two cases, popular. A play like Samuel Beckett's *Waiting for Godot* seemed at one time to be incomprehensible to managers, directors and public alike. When it was first staged, people walked out in protest. Yet nowadays repertory companies and amateur groups play it all over the country. When Harold Pinter's *The Birthday Party* was originally presented in 1958, it was forced to close in less than a week. But Pinter is now a highly successful and, what is more, a widely imitated dramatist. His play *The Caretaker* ran for months in the West End of London, and then in New York on Broadway, and has done equally well as a film.

Something like a revolution, in fact, has happened in the theatre, and it has changed many of our settled ideas about what a good play should be like, what sort of things it can say, how it should say them, and what we consider 'entertaining'. The present selection of one-act plays attempts to reflect something of this change, and to introduce young readers to a few of the dramatists who are responsible for it. This is not, however, a volume of self-consciously *avant-garde* drama. It would be absurd to think of modern theatre exclusively in such terms, or to suppose that the only worth-while drama being written nowadays is of an unconventional kind. Plays like *Hall of Healing* or *The Oyster and the Pearl* have nothing 'experimental' about them. Their value and their modernity lie in what they have to say, not in any novel way of saying it. On the other hand, one or two of these plays may well appear, on first acquaintance, puzzling or 'difficult'. What they are getting at may not be immediately clear, and the way they are written may not conform to the normal definition of good dialogue or of a good theatrical situation. Each play here has been given a short introduction of its own, to provide some guidance where individual difficulties of meaning or interpretation may arise. But it is worth looking first in a more general way at some of the unfamiliar characteristics of the more 'modern' sort of drama, and at how conventions as a whole have changed in the modern theatre.

The most fundamental change has been one of style, and it has been caused by a steady movement away from the methods of naturalism and realism. Though the effects of it have been particularly noticeable since the last war, and have in fact only become influential in the English theatre itself over the past decade, this movement is something which has been taking place in all the arts, not only in the theatre, during the last fifty

years. At the beginning of the present century the domi-
nant dramatic style was that practised by such writers
as Ibsen and Tchekov, whose plays were really theatrical
extensions of the great nineteenth century tradition of
the novel. Their themes depended on the exploration
of character, they told a straightforward story about
recognisable types of people, and they were acted on
stages which were detailed replicas of actual life. In a
rather tired form, this tradition is still very much with
us, particularly in the typical 'well-made' West End play.
The curtain goes up on a comfortably furnished drawing-
room, or some equally familiar setting, and we watch a
plot being acted out much as it might happen in reality.
It is what has been called 'fourth-wall' drama: the only
thing we are asked to imagine is that the proscenium
arch is the fourth wall of a room and that through it
we are able to watch what happens inside. One un-
doubted reason why there should be a reaction against
this naturalistic, or realistic, tradition, has been the
cinema, reinforced nowadays by the effects of television.
The cinema has proved conclusively that it can depict
real life much more authentically than the theatre would
ever be able to do, just as the camera proved to painters
that it could 'represent' the natural appearance of things
more quickly and accurately than they could. In the
theatre, as in modern painting, the literal depiction of
events or of nature began, therefore, to give way to more
imaginative or symbolic renderings of them. Dramatists
began to argue that what happened on a stage was not 'real'
anyhow, but acting, and pretence, and illusion, and that it
was artistically dishonest to pretend otherwise. And these
arguments have had a marked effect on modern stage
practice. The whole style of presentation tends now towards underlining, not concealing, the fact that a

play is a form of pretence—actors pretend to be people other than themselves; they pretend to hold conversations which have actually been written for them in advance and carefully rehearsed. There are continual attempts now to break away from the 'picture-frame' stage (the 'realistic' sort of stage where actors behave as if there were no audience watching them) towards the 'apron' stage, the 'arena' stage, 'theatre in the round', and so on, which are all forms of staging which bring actors and audience into closer contact with each other and emphasize that a play is a performance and not real life. Scenery and settings, too, following the same trend, have become much less illusionistic and less elaborate. In fact, there is a fondness now for leaving the stage almost bare, so that everything is made to depend on the audience's imagination and the actor's power of suggestion. *It Should Happen to a Dog* and *Then...* are good examples of this bare, purely functional way of staging plays. Adequate floor space and enough lighting to create atmosphere are all they require.

'Functional' staging—the reverse of realism and illusion—is nothing new, of course. It is what Shakespeare refers to in the prologue to *Henry V,* when the Chorus speaks of 'this unworthy scaffold' (the stage) and invites the audience to create the setting of the play for themselves in imagination:

For 'tis your thoughts that now must deck our kings,
Carry them here and there, jumping o'er times,
Turning the accomplishment of many years
Into an hour-glass....

The open stage for Shakespeare was a way of harnessing imagination to the swift and vivid telling of a story covering a wide field of action. But when we come to certain types of modern play, we find that, though they are still calling on us to use our imaginations, a story, as such, is not what they are usually concerned to tell.[1] *Waiting for Godot* was itself notorious because nothing 'happened' in it. At the end you were no further forward than you had been at the beginning. The play seemed to be shapeless, to have no plot or climax. The two little Pinter plays in this volume are of the same kind, while the 'plots' of *The New Tenant* and *The Sandbox*, though they have a clear shape, are certainly not straightforward stories. Perhaps the simplest way to account for this is to draw an analogy with the difference between prose fiction and poetry. 'Traditional' plays, as was suggested above about naturalistic drama in general, are like the theatrical equivalent of novels, in which there is a logical sequence of events towards a satisfying resolution or dénouement. But certain modern dramatists are writing what are virtually poems for the theatre. This does not mean that they write in verse. But it does mean they are trying to say things which cannot be expressed in ordinary prose terms. They make use of fantasy, symbolism and poetic imagery—an entire 'plot' may itself be a symbol or an image—and their full meaning can only be grasped by the imagination, as poetry is, rather than by logic or reason. What this implies in *The New Tenant* and *The Sandbox* is more fully discussed in the indivi-

---

[1] Though exception must be made of the great German playwright, Bertolt Brecht, whose work unfortunately could not be represented in this volume for copyright reasons. Brecht's aim was always to tell a story, and one with a definite moral to it. His plays, with their forceful, direct expression, episodic construction and evocatively simple staging, have become widely influential, affecting in this country the plays of John Osborne, John Arden, Arnold Wesker, and the productions of Joan Littlewood, etc.

dual prefaces to these two plays. Pinter's plays are rather different, though they can still be compared to a certain kind of poem. For example:

> the black wings
> of the
>
> hospital where
> nothing
>
> will grow lie
> cinders
>
> in which shine
> the broken
>
> pieces of a green
> bottle

which is a complete poem by William Carlos Williams. They do not use symbols or metaphors. But they take a tiny, seemingly insignificant fragment of experience; hold it up, as it were, for our inspection; and by the exactness and economy with which they describe it, they make it *exist* for us more vividly than it could before. The pauses in them are, in one way, like the pauses in ordinary life, when the speaker has nothing more in particular to say, or is just mentally resting. But they are also like the pauses in music, or between the verses of a poem: they are part of a rhythmic structure which is essential to the whole.

To talk in such terms about such plays, however, may sound odd when a more obvious thing about them is their humour (both *The Black and White* and *Last to Go* were originally acted as scenes in a revue). And an important aspect of a great deal of modern drama is the sort of humour expressed in it, because it is not unrelated to the whole trend towards fantasy and anti-realism. Usually it is often not a humour that depends on jokes or witty lines at all, in the ordinary sense. It is much closer to the dream-like illogicality of Lewis Carroll or the nonsense of Edward Lear. In Pinter it breaks out in the apparent *non-sequiturs* of conversation when two people are following slightly different lines of thought. But in a writer like N. F. Simpson, the author of *One Way Pendulum* and *A Resounding Tinkle* (titles with connotations of absurdity in themselves), illogicality is deliberately carried to extravagant lengths. There is, for example, the famous opening scene of *One Way Pendulum*, in which the hero is discovered trying to conduct a choir of weighing machines in the Hallelujah Chorus. This is exactly the same sort of nonsense humour as that of the Marx Brothers or The Goon Show, and is exactly that of George Bernard Shaw in *Passion, Poison and Petrifaction*, which represents that form of humour in this volume.

The use of illogical, fantastic situations in modern drama, however, goes further than the purposes of humour alone. It amounts almost to a way of interpreting the world we live in. One could say, for example, that ours is an age which no longer believes in the primacy of reason as other ages have believed in it. The twentieth century has experienced, to a large degree, the breakdown of man's faith in himself as a logical being. Psychology has taught us how much we are governed by unconscious impulses. Two world wars have shown us nations gone mad. Even science, for all the wonders of its achievement, has confounded us with the assertion that space is curved, and has presented us with a convenient means for wiping ourselves off the face of the earth. This is the tragedy of our age, but also the absurdity of it. The times are out of joint. Lunacy— whether you react to the word in its serious or its comic sense—prevails. That, at any rate, is how many writers and thinkers interpret our present world. And in drama this attitude of mind has given rise to two very characteristic types of play, one of which is known as the Theatre of the Absurd, and the other as the Comedy of Menace.

The Theatre of the Absurd is particularly associated with the work of Eugène Ionesco, who is represented in this volume by *The New Tenant*. *The New Tenant* has moments of goon-like fantasy—when the furniture-removers, for example, carry-in a vase as if it weighed as much as a wardrobe, or when the pile-up of furniture outside starts blocking the Underground and damming the Thames. But if, in a literal sense, the play's plot is absurd, in a symbolic or poetic sense it is deeply disturbing, for it gives a graphic image of how a man can cut himself off from the world he lives in. Behind a great deal of the surface absurdity of plays like Ionesco's, there lie intimations of much deeper, more tragic, issues. The Comedy of Menace deals with a specific, more limited area of this same territory. Its concern is with the kind of comic situation which makes one's nerves tingle because behind it lurks fear—the fear of violence, the fear of Orwell's *1984*, or the fear, as in the play by David Campton in this volume, of The Bomb itself. These are concerns which loom particularly large in the mid-twentieth century, and affect all our lives directly or indirectly. Plays like Ionesco's or David Campton's may not be preaching at us quite as O'Casey's *Hall of Healing* does, with its cry of rage at a whole pack of social injustices and abuses. But they carry, nevertheless, a serious 'message' which is a comment on us and our times.

In this volume are plays which come from Europe

xiv

and America as well as from Britain. The Theatre of the Absurd is itself more a European phenomenon than an English one, while Comedy of Menace is a term that was invented in England, though there are dramatists abroad to whose work it could equally well apply. The theatre is an international art in spite of the barriers of language, and since the last war the three writers who have most influenced the sort of drama that has been discussed here—Ionesco, Brecht and Beckett—happen to be Rumanian, German and Irish respectively (though both Ionesco and Beckett work in Paris). But in England there is a special reason for being aware of such influences now, for the English theatre has acquired a new look and a new creative vitality ever since that historic night of 8 May 1956 when John Osborne's *Look Back in Anger* had its first performance. A whole new generation of writers—John Arden, Arnold Wesker, Harold Pinter, N. F. Simpson, Alun Owen, David Campton and many others—suddenly sprang into prominence following Osborne's success, and they have, over the past few years, virtually created a new theatregoing public and given a wholly fresh impetus to modern drama in this country.[1] The present selection can only hint at the new fields that have been opened up, but it will have achieved its purpose if it can suggest to this generation the range and interest and stimulation of new ideas to be found in the theatre today.

*1965*                                    DAVID THOMPSON

[1] A detailed account of this 'revolution' can be found in John Russell Taylor's book *Anger and After* (Pelican Books) and a wider-ranging study of it in Lawrence Kitchin's *Mid-Century Drama* (Faber and Faber).

# Passion, Poison, and Petrifaction
## *or*
# The Fatal Gazogene

*Bernard Shaw (1856-1950)*

## Characters

Lady Magnesia Fitztollemache
Phyllis—*her maid*
George Fitztollemache—*the murderer*
Adolphus Bastable
Landlord
Policeman
Doctor

## EDITOR'S NOTE

Bernard Shaw said his fatal weakness was an inability to resist clowning. Nevertheless, he rarely let himself go in quite such a farce as this, which is one of a group of *jeux d'esprit* he called 'tomfooleries'. Essentially it is a wild caricature of the sort of Victorian melodrama that was by no means yet extinct when he himself started writing. But the reason for including it here, apart from the fact that it is very funny, is to suggest that the modern 'Theatre of the Absurd' (see Introduction) is not as 'modern' as all that. Shaw strikes almost exactly the same note of surrealistic nonsense in this play as that of Ionesco in many of his, or of an English dramatist like N. F. Simpson in *A Resounding Tinkle* (1956) or *One Way Pendulum* (1959). It is a nonsense which, like all the best nonsense, behaves with a grotesque logic of its own. Dreamlike improbabilities are accepted with poker-faced gravity by the characters concerned as if they were the most natural things in the world. Notice, too, Shaw's inventiveness with the theatrical *medium*. He revels in opportunities for reminding the audience where they are (compare, for instance, his use of the theatre-attendants at the very end with Grandma's quite open instructions to the stage-electrician in Albee's *The Sandbox* later in this volume).

However, good jokes should not be talked about but left to speak for themselves. It is enough to say that a gazogene is what we would nowadays call a soda-siphon, and that 'Won't you come home, Bill Bailey?' was a popular ballad of about 1905 (when the play was written). But the joke is best sustained if the latest hit-tune is substituted for it. A thunder-sheet, a spotlight with a simple colour-wheel, and native ingenuity can cope with most of the effects in practical performance.

# PASSION, POISON, AND PETRIFACTION
## or
## THE FATAL GAZOGENE

*In a bed-sitting room in a fashionable quarter of London a lady sits at her dressing-table, with her maid combing her hair. It is late; and the electric lamps are glowing. Apparently the room is bedless; but there stands against the opposite wall to that at which the dressing-table is placed a piece of furniture that suggests a bookcase without carrying conviction. On the same side is a chest of drawers of that disastrous kind which, recalcitrant to the opener until she is provoked to violence, then suddenly come wholly out and defy all her efforts to fit them in again. Opposite this chest of drawers, on the lady's side of the room, is a cupboard. The presence of a row of gentleman's boots beside the chest of drawers proclaims that the lady is married. Her own boots are beside the cupboard. The third wall is pierced midway by the door, above which is a cuckoo clock. Near the door a pedestal bears a portrait bust of the lady in plaster. There is a fan on the dressing-table, a hatbox and rug-strap on the chest of drawers, an umbrella and a bootjack against the wall near the bed. The general impression is one of brightness, beauty and social ambition, damped by somewhat inadequate means. A certain air of theatricality is produced by the fact that though the room is rectangular it has only three walls. Not a sound is heard except the overture and the crackling of the lady's hair as the maid's brush draws electric sparks from it in the dry air of the London midsummer. The cuckoo clock strikes sixteen.*

LADY: How much did the clock strike, Phyllis?

PHYLLIS: Sixteen, my lady.

LADY: That means eleven o'clock, does it not?

PHYLLIS: Eleven at night, my lady. In the morning it means half-past two; so if you hear it strike sixteen during your slumbers, do not rise.

LADY: I will not Phyllis. Phyllis—I am weary. I will go to bed. Prepare my couch.

PHYLLIS *crosses the room to the bookcase and touches a button. The front of the bookcase falls out with a crash and becomes a bed. A roll of distant thunder echoes the crash.*

PHYLLIS (*shuddering*): It is a terrible night. Heaven help all poor mariners at sea! My master is late. I trust nothing has happened to him. Your bed is ready, my lady.

LADY: Thank you, Phyllis. (*She rises and approaches the bed*) Goodnight.

PHYLLIS: Will your ladyship not undress?

LADY: Not tonight, Phyllis. (*Glancing through where the fourth wall is missing, at the audience*) Not under the circumstances.

PHYLLIS (*impulsively throwing herself on her knees by her mistress's side and clasping her round the waist*): Oh, my beloved mistress, I know not why or how; but I feel that I shall never see you alive again. There is murder in the air. (*Thunder*) Hark!

LADY: Strange! As I sat there methought I heard angels singing, 'Oh, won't you come home, Bill Bailey?' Why should angels call me Bill Bailey? My name is Magnesia Fitztollemache.

PHYLLIS (*emphasizing the title*): *Lady* Magnesia Fitztollemache.

5

LADY: In case we should never again meet in this world, let us take a last farewell.

PHYLLIS (*embracing her with tears*): My poor murdered angel mistress!

LADY: In case we *should* meet again, call me at half-past eleven.

PHYLLIS: I will, I will.

> PHYLLIS *withdraws, overcome by emotion.* LADY MAGNESIA *switches off the electric light and immediately hears the angels quite distinctly. They sing, 'Bill Bailey' so sweetly that she can attend to nothing else, and forgets to remove even her boots as she draws the coverlet over herself and sinks to sleep, lulled by celestial harmony. A white radiance plays upon her pillow, and lights up her beautiful face. But the thunder growls again; and a lurid red glow concentrates itself on the door, which is presently flung open, revealing a saturnine figure in evening dress, partially concealed by a crimson cloak. As he steals towards the bed the unnatural glare in his eyes and the broad-bladed dagger nervously gripped in his right hand bode ill for the sleeping lady. Providentially she sneezes on the very brink of eternity; and the tension of the murderer's nerves is such that he bolts precipitately under the bed at the sudden and startling* Atscha! *A dull, heavy rhythmic thumping—the beating of his heart—betrays his whereabouts. Soon he emerges cautiously and raises his head above the bed coverlet level.*

MURDERER: I can no longer cower here listening to the agonized thumpings of my own heart. She but snoze in her sleep. I'll do it. (*He again raises the dagger. The angels sing again. He cowers*) What is this? Has that tune reached Heaven?

MAGNESIA (*waking and sitting up*): My husband! (*All the colours of the rainbow chase one another up his face with ghastly brilliancy.*) Why do you change colour? And what on earth are you doing with that dagger?

FITZ (*affecting unconcern, but unhinged*): It is a present for you: a present from mother. Pretty, isn't it? (*he displays it fatuously*)

MAGNESIA: But she promised me a fish slice.

FITZ: This is a combination fish slice and dagger. One day you have salmon for dinner. The next you have a murder to commit. See?

MAGNESIA: My sweet mother-in-law! (*Someone knocks at the door.*) That is Adolphus's knock (FITZ's face turns a *dazzling green.*) What has happened to your complexion? You have turned green. Now I think of it, you always do when Adolphus is mentioned. Aren't you going to let him in?

FITZ: Certainly not. (*He goes to the door*) Adolphus: you cannot enter. My wife is undressed and in bed.

MAGNESIA (*rising*): I am not. Come in, Adolphus (*she switches on the electric light*).

ADOLPHUS (*without*): Something most important has happened. I must come in for a moment.

FITZ (*calling to* ADOLPHUS): Something important happened? What is it?

ADOLPHUS (*without*): My new clothes have come home.

FITZ: He says his new clothes have come home.

MAGNESIA (*running to the door and opening it*): Oh, come in. Let me see.

ADOLPHUS BASTABLE *enters. He is in evening dress, made in the latest fashion, with the right half of the coat and the left half of the trousers yellow and the other halves black. His silver-spangled waistcoat has a crimson handkerchief stuck between it and his shirt front.*

7

ADOLPHUS: What do you think of it?

MAGNESIA: It is a dream! a creation! (*she turns him about to admire him*).

ADOLPHUS (*proudly*): I shall never be mistaken for a waiter again.

FITZ: A drink, Adolphus?

ADOLPHUS: Thanks.

> FITZTOLLEMACHE *goes to the cupboard and takes out a tray with tumblers and a bottle of whisky. He puts them on the dressing-table.*

FITZ: Is the gazogene full?

MAGNESIA: Yes: you put in the powders yourself today.

FITZ (*sardonically*): So I did. The special powders! Ha! Ha! Ha! Ha! Ha! (*his face is again strangely variegated*)

MAGNESIA: Your complexion is really going to pieces. Why do you laugh in that silly way at nothing?

FITZ: Nothing! Ha, ha! Nothing? Ha, ha, ha!

ADOLPHUS: I hope, Mr Fitztollemache, you are not laughing at my clothes. I warn you that I am an Englishman. You may laugh at my manners, at my brains, at my national institutions; but if you laugh at my clothes, one of us must die.

*Thunder.*

FITZ: I laughed but at the irony of Fate. (*he takes a gazogene from the cupboard*).

ADOLPHUS (*satisfied*): Oh, *that*! Oh, yes, of course!

FITZ: Let us drown all unkindness in a loving cup. (*He puts the gazogene on the floor in the middle of the room*). Pardon the absence of a table: we found it in the way and pawned it. (*He takes the whisky bottle from the dressing-table*)

MAGNESIA: We picnic at home now. It is delightful.

*She takes three tumblers from the dressing-table and sits
on the floor, presiding over the gazogene, with* FITZ *and*
ADOLPHUS *squatting on her left and right respectively.*
FITZ *pours whisky into the tumblers.*

FITZ (*as* MAGNESIA *is about to squirt soda into his tumbler*):
Stay! No soda for me. Let Adolphus have it all—*all*.
I will take mine neat.

MAGNESIA (*proffering tumbler to* ADOLPHUS): Pledge me,
Adolphus.

FITZ: Kiss the cup, Magnesia. Pledge her, man. Drink
deep.

ADOLPHUS: To Magnesia!

FITZ: To Magnesia! (*The two men drink*) It is done.
(*Scrambling to his feet*) Adolphus: you have but ten
minutes to live—if so long.

ADOLPHUS: What mean you?

MAGNESIA (*rising*): My mind misgives me. I have a strange
feeling here (*touching her heart*).

ADOLPHUS: So have I, but lower down (*touching his
stomach*). That gazogene is disagreeing with me.

FITZ: It was poisoned.

*Sensation.*

ADOLPHUS (*rising*): Help! Police!

FITZ: Dastard! you would appeal to the law? Can you not
die like a gentleman?

ADOLPHUS: But so young? when I have only worn my new
clothes once.

MAGNESIA: It is too horrible. (*To* FITZ) Fiend! what drove
you to this wicked deed?

FITZ: Jealousy. You admired his clothes: you did not
admire mine.

ADOLPHUS: My clothes! (*his face lights up with heavenly
radiance*). Have I indeed been found worthy to be the

9

first clothes-martyr? Welcome, death! Hark! angels call me. (*The celestial choir again raises its favourite chant. He listens with a rapt expression. Suddenly the angels sing out of tune; and the radiance on the poisoned man's face turns a sickly green.*) Yah-ah! Oh-ahoo! The gazogene is disagreeing extremely. Oh! (*he throws himself on the bed, writhing*).

MAGNESIA (*to* FITZ): Monster; what have you done? (*She points to the distorted figure on the bed*) That was once a Man, beautiful and glorious. What have you made of it? A writhing, agonized, miserable, moribund worm.

ADOLPHUS (*in a tone of the strongest remonstrance*): Oh, I say! Oh, come! Now look here, Magnesia! Really!

MAGNESIA: Oh, is this a time for petty vanity? Think of your misspent life—

ADOLPHUS (*much injured*): *Whose* misspent life?

MAGNESIA (*continuing relentlessly*): Look into your conscience: look into your stomach. (ADOLPHUS *collapses in hideous spasms. She turns to* FITZ) And this is *your* handiwork!

FITZ: Mine is a passionate nature, Magnesia. I must have your undivided love. I must have your love: do you hear me? LOVE! LOVE!! LOVE!!! LOVE!!!! LOVE!!!!!

*He raves, accompanied by a fresh paroxysm from the victim on the bed.*

MAGNESIA (*with sudden resolution*): You *shall* have it.

FITZ (*enraptured*): Magnesia! I have recovered your love! Oh, how slight appears the sacrifice of this man compared to so glorious a reward! I would poison ten men without a thought of self to gain one smile from you.

ADOLPHUS (*in a broken voice*): Farewell, Magnesia: my last hour is at hand. Farewell, farewell, farewell!

MAGNESIA: At this supreme moment, George Fitztolle-mache, I solemnly dedicate to you all that I formerly dedicated to poor Adolphus.

ADOLPHUS: Oh, please not poor Adolphus yet. I still live, you know.

MAGNESIA: The vital spark but flashes before it vanishes. (ADOLPHUS *groans*). And now, Adolphus, take this last comfort from the unhappy Magnesia Fitztollemache. As I have dedicated to George all that I gave to you, so I will bury in your grave—or in your urn if you are cremated—all that I gave to him.

FITZ: I hardly follow this.

MAGNESIA: I will explain. George: hitherto I have given Adolphus all the romance of my nature—all my love—all my dreams—all my caresses. Henceforth they are yours!

FITZ: Angel!

MAGNESIA: Adolphus: forgive me if this pains you.

ADOLPHUS: Don't mention it. I hardly feel it. The gazogene is so much worse. (*Taken bad again*) Oh!

MAGNESIA: Peace, poor sufferer: there is still some balm. You are about to hear what I am going to dedicate to *you.*

ADOLPHUS: All I ask is a peppermint lozenge, for mercy's sake.

MAGNESIA: I have something far better than any lozenge: the devotion of a lifetime. Formerly it was George's. I kept his house, or rather, his lodgings. I mended his clothes. I darned his socks. I bought his food. I inter-viewed his creditors. I stood between him and the ser-vants. I administered his domestic finances. When his hair needed cutting or his countenance was imperfectly washed, I pointed it out to him. The trouble that all this gave me made him prosaic in my eyes. Familiarity

11

bred contempt. Now all that shall end. My husband shall be my hero, my lover, my perfect knight. He shall shield me from all care and trouble. He shall ask nothing in return but love—boundless, priceless, rapturous, soul enthralling love, LOVE! LOVE!! LOVE!!! (*she raves, flinging her arms about* FITZ). And the duties I formerly discharged shall be replaced by the one supreme duty of duties: the duty of weeping at Adolphus's tomb.

FITZ (*reflectively*): My ownest, this sacrifice makes me feel that I have perhaps been a little selfish. I cannot help feeling that there is much to be said for the old arrangement. Why should Adolphus die for my sake?

ADOLPHUS: I am not dying for your sake, Fitz. I am dying because you poisoned me.

MAGNESIA: You do not fear to die, Adolphus, do you?

ADOLPHUS: N-n-no, I don't exactly fear to die. Still—

FITZ: Still, if an antidote—

ADOLPHUS (*bounding from the bed*): Antidote!

FITZ: If an antidote would not be too much of an anti-climax.

ADOLPHUS: Anti-climax be blowed; Do you think I am going to die to please the critics? Out with your antidote. Quick!

FITZ: The best antidote to the poison I have given you is lime, plenty of lime.

ADOLPHUS: Lime! You mock me! Do you think I carry lime about in my pockets?

FITZ: There is the plaster ceiling.

MAGNESIA: Yes, the ceiling. Saved, saved, saved!

*All three frantically shy boots at the ceiling. Flakes of plaster rain down which* ADOLPHUS *devours, at first ravenously, then with a marked falling off in relish.*

MAGNESIA (*picking up a huge slice*): Take this Adolphus: it is the largest (*she crams it into his mouth*).

FITZ: Ha! a lump off the cornice! Try this.

ADOLPHUS (*desperately*): Stop! Stop!

MAGNESIA: Do not stop. You will die. (*She tries to stuff him again*).

ADOLPHUS (*resolutely*): I prefer death.

MAGNESIA and FITZ (*throwing themselves on their knees on either side of him*): For our sakes, Adolphus, persevere.

ADOLPHUS: No: unless you can supply lime in liquid form, I must perish. Finish that ceiling I cannot and will not.

MAGNESIA: I have a thought—an inspiration. My bust. (*She snatches it from its pedestal and brings it to him*).

ADOLPHUS (*gazing fondly at it*): Can I resist it?

FITZ: Try the bun.

ADOLPHUS (*gnawing the knot of hair at the back of the bust's head: it makes him ill*): Yah, I cannot. I cannot. Not even *your* bust, Magnesia. Do not ask me. Let me die.

FITZ (*pressing the bust on him*): Force yourself to take a mouthful. Down with it, Adolphus.

ADOLPHUS: Useless. It would not stay down. Water! Some fluid! Ring for something to drink (*he chokes*).

MAGNESIA: I will save you (*she rushes to the bell and rings*).

PHYLLIS, *in her night-gown, with her hair prettily made up into a chevaux de frise of crocuses with pink and yellow curl papers, rushes in straight to* MAGNESIA.

PHYLLIS (*hysterically*): My beloved mistress, once more we meet (*She sees* FITZTOLLEMACHE *and screams*) Ah! Ah! Ah! A man! (*She sees* ADOLPHUS) Men!! (*She flies; but* FITZ *seizes her by the night-gown just as she is escaping*). Unhand me, villain!

13

FITZ: This is no time for prudery, girl. Mr Bastable is dying.

PHYLLIS (*with concern*): Indeed, sir? I hope he will not think it unfeeling of me to appear at his deathbed in curl papers.

MAGNESIA: We know you have a good heart, Phyllis. Take this (*giving her the bust*); dissolve it in a jug of hot water; and bring it back instantly. Mr Bastable's life depends on your haste.

PHYLLIS (*hesitating*): It do seem a pity, don't it, my lady, to spoil your lovely bust.

ADOLPHUS: Tush! This craze for fine art is beyond all bounds. Off with you (*he pushes her out*). Drink, drink, drink! My entrails are parched. Drink! (*he rushes deliriously to the gazogene*).

FITZ (*rushing after him*): Madman, you forget! It is poisoned!

ADOLPHUS: I don't care. Drink, drink! (*They wrestle madly for the gazogene. In the struggle they squirt all its contents away, mostly into one another's faces.* ADOLPHUS *at last flings* FITZTOLLEMACHE *to the floor and puts the spout into his mouth.*) Empty! empty! (*with a shriek of despair he collapses on the bed, clasping the gazogene like a baby, and weeping over it*).

FITZ (*aside to* MAGNESIA): Magnesia: I have always pretended not to notice it; but you keep a siphon for your private use in my hat-box.

MAGNESIA: I use it for washing old lace. But no matter: he shall have it (*she produces a siphon from the hat-box, and offers a tumbler of soda-water to* ADOLPHUS).

ADOLPHUS: Thanks, thanks, oh, thanks! (*he drinks. A terrific fizzing is heard. He starts up screaming*) Help! Help! The ceiling is effervescing! I am BURSTING! (*He wallows convulsively on the bed*).

FITZ: Quick! The rug strap! (*They pack him with blankets and strap him*). Is that tight enough?

MAGNESIA (*anxiously*): Will you hold, do you think?

ADOLPHUS: The peril is past. The soda-water has gone flat.

MAGNESIA and FITZ: Thank heaven!

PHYLLIS *returns with a washstand ewer, in which she has dissolved the bust.*

MAGNESIA (*snatching it*): At last!

FITZ: You are saved. Drain it to the dregs.

FITZ *holds the lip of the ewer to* ADOLPHUS's *mouth and gradually raises it until it stands upside down.* ADOLPHUS's *efforts to swallow it are fearful,* PHYLLIS *thumping his back when he chokes, and* MAGNESIA *loosening the straps when he moans. At last, with a sigh of relief, he sinks back in the women's arms.* FITZ *shakes the empty ewer upside down like a potman shaking the froth out of a flagon.*

ADOLPHUS: How inexpressibly soothing to the chest! A delicious numbness steals through all my members. I would sleep.

MAGNESIA  
FITZ  } (*whispering*): Let him sleep.  
PHYLLIS

*He sleeps. Celestial harps are heard; but their chords cease on the abrupt entrance of the landlord, a vulgar person in pyjamas.*

LANDLORD: Eah! Eah! Wots this? Wots all this noise? Ah kin ennybody sleep through it? (*Looking at the floor and ceiling*) Ellow! wot you bin doin te maw ceilin?

FITZ: Silence, or leave the room. If you wake that man he dies.

LANDLORD: If e kin sleep through the noise you three mikes e kin sleep through ennythink.

MAGNESIA: Detestable vulgarian: your pronunciation jars on the finest chords of my nature. Begone!

LANDLORD (*looking at* ADOLPHUS): Aw d-ownt blieve eze esleep. Aw blieve eze dead. (*Calling*) Pleece! Pleece! Merder! (*A blue halo plays mysteriously on the door, which opens and reveals a policeman. Thunder*). Eah, pleecmin: these three's bin an merdered this gent between em, an naw tore moy ahse dahn.

POLICEMAN (*offended*): Policeman, indeed! Where's your manners.

FITZ: Officer—

POLICEMAN (*with distinguished consideration*): Sir?

FITZ: As between gentlemen—

POLICEMAN (*bowing*): Sir: to you.

FITZ (*bowing*): I may inform you that my friend had an acute attack of indigestion. No carbonate of soda being available, he swallowed a portion of this man's ceiling. (*Pointing to* ADOLPHUS) Behold the result!

POLICEMAN: The ceiling was poisoned! Well, of all the artful—(*he collars the* LANDLORD). I arrest you for wilful murder.

LANDLORD (*appealing to the heavens*): Ow, is this jestice! Ah could aw tell e wiz gowin to eat moy ceiling?

POLICEMAN (*releasing him*): True. The case is more complicated than I thought. (*He tries to lift* ADOLPHUS'S *arm but cannot*). Stiff already.

LANDLORD (*trying to lift* ADOLPHUS'S *leg*): And precious evvy (*Feeling the calf*) Woy, eze gorn ez awd ez niles.

FITZ (*rushing to the bed*): What is this?

MAGNESIA: Oh, say he is not dead. Phyllis: fetch a doctor.

(PHYLLIS *runs out. They all try to lift* ADOLPHUS; *but he is perfectly stiff and as heavy as lead*). Rouse him. Shake him.

POLICEMAN (*exhausted*): Whew! Is he a man or a statue? (MAGNESIA *utters a piercing scream*). What's wrong, Miss?

MAGNESIA (*to* FITZ): Do you not see what has happened?

FITZ (*striking his forehead*): Horror on horror's head!

LANDLORD: Wotjemean?

MAGNESIA: The plaster has set inside him. The officer was right: he is indeed a living statue.

MAGNESIA *flings herself on the stony breast of* ADOLPHUS. FITZ *buries his head in his hands; and his chest heaves convulsively. The* POLICEMAN *takes a small volume from his pocket and consults it.*

POLICEMAN: This case is not provided for in my book of instructions. It don't seem no use trying artificial respiration, do it? (*To the* LANDLORD) Here, lend a hand, you. We'd best take him and set him up in Trafalgar Square.

LANDLORD: Aushd pat im in the cestern an worsh it aht of im.

PHYLLIS *comes back with a* DOCTOR.

PHYLLIS: The medical man, my lady.

POLICEMAN: A poison case, sir.

DOCTOR: Do you mean to say that an unqualified person! a layman! has dared to administer poison in my district?

POLICEMAN (*raising* MAGNESIA *tenderly*): It looks like it. Hold up, my lady.

DOCTOR: Not a moment must be lost. The patient must be kept awake at all costs. Constant and violent motion is necessary.

*He snatches* MAGNESIA *from the* POLICEMAN, *and rushes her about the room.*

FITZ: Stop! That is not the poisoned person!

DOCTOR: Is it you, then. Why did you not say so before?

*He seizes* FITZ *and rushes him about.*

LANDLORD: Naow, naow, thet ynt im.

DOCTOR: What, you!

*He pounces on the landlord and rushes him round.*

LANDLORD: Eah! chack it. (*He trips the* DOCTOR *up. Both fall*). Jest owld this leeonatic, will you, Mister Horficer?

POLICEMAN (*dragging both of them to their feet*): Come out of it, will you. You must all come with me to the station.

*Thunder.*

MAGNESIA: What! In this frightful storm!

*The hail patters noisily on the window.*

PHYLLIS: I think it's raining.

*The wind howls.*

LANDLORD: It's thanderin and lawtnin.

FITZ: It's dangerous.

POLICEMAN (*drawing his baton and whistle*): If you won't come quietly, then—

*He whistles. A fearful flash is followed by an appalling explosion of heaven's artillery. A thunderbolt enters the room, and strikes the helmet of the devoted* CONSTABLE, *whence it is attracted to the waistcoat of the* DOCTOR *by the lancet in his pocket. Finally it leaps with fearful force on the* LANDLORD, *who, being of a gross and spongy nature, absorbs the electric fluid at the cost of his life. The others look on horror-stricken as the three victims, after reeling, jostling, cannoning through a ghastly quadrille, at last sink inanimate on the carpet.*

18

MAGNESIA (*listening at the* DOCTOR's *chest*): Dead!

FITZ (*kneeling by the* LANDLORD, *and raising his hand, which drops with a thud*): Dead!

PHYLLIS (*seizing the looking-glass and holding it to the* POLICEMAN's *lips*): Dead!

FITZ (*solemnly rising*): The copper attracted the lightning.

MAGNESIA (*rising*): After life's fitful fever they sleep well. Phyllis sweep them up.

PHYLLIS *replaces the looking-glass on the dressing-table; takes up the fan; and fans the* POLICEMAN, *who rolls away like a leaf before the wind to the wall. She disposes similarly of the* LANDLORD *and* DOCTOR.

PHYLLIS: Will they be in your way if I leave them there until morning, my lady? Or shall I bring up the ashpan and take them away?

MAGNESIA: They will not disturb us. Goodnight, Phyllis.

PHYLLIS: Goodnight, my lady. Goodnight, sir.

*She retires.*

MAGNESIA: And now, husband, let us perform our last duty to our friend. He has become his own monument. Let us erect him. He is heavy; but love can do much.

FITZ: A little leverage will get him on his feet. Give me my umbrella.

MAGNESIA: True.

*She hands him the umbrella, and takes up the boot-jack. They get them under* ADOLPHUS's *back, and prize him up on his feet.*

FITZ: That's done it! Whew!

MAGNESIA (*kneeling at the left hand of the statue*): For ever and ever, Adolphus.

FITZ (*kneeling at the right hand of the statue*): The rest is silence.

*The Angels sing Bill Bailey. The statue raises its hands in an attitude of blessing, and turns its limelit face to heaven as the curtain falls. National Anthem.*

ATTENDANTS (*in front*): All out for the next performance. Pass along, please, ladies and gentlemen: pass along.

# Hall of Healing

## A Sincerious Farce in One Scene

*Sean O'Casey (1880-1964)*

## Characters

Alleluia (Aloysius), the Caretaker of the Dispensary
The Old Woman ⎫
The Young
    Woman
Black Muffler ⎬ patients attending the Dispensary
Green Muffler
Jentree ⎭
A Lad
The Doctor, the Dispensary's Medical Officer
The Apothecary, the Dispensary's Dispenser
Red Muffler
Grey Shawl, Red Muffler's wife

# EDITOR'S NOTE

O'Casey calls this a 'sincerious farce', but it is not Shaw's kind of farce in *Passion, Poison and Petrifaction*, for both the words implied in 'sincerious' must be taken literally. *Hall of Healing*, in fact, is a highly characteristic example of the sort of writing for which O'Casey is famous. It is an inextricable mixture of comedy and tragedy, and both elements should be allowed to come out strongly in the acting. The tragedy is in the setting and the situation, and it is brought to a head by the final incident of the play. The comedy is all in the characterization and dialogue, particularly in the extravagantly colourful turns of speech. Getting the Irish accent right is much less important here than catching the general rhythm and relishing O'Casey's language to the full. It is his way of expressing how rich and genial human nature insists on being, even when all the cards are stacked against it.

Though O'Casey left Ireland for good in the 1920s, his plays always tend to refer back to the troubled period of Irish history he had just lived through in Dublin, and he gives to this particular situation a universal significance. The joy of life and everybody's right to it are the constant themes of his later plays, and he is forever lashing out at social or political conditions that, in his view, deny that basic joy. Both the profession of medicine and the hypocrisy of certain people who call themselves 'religious' are the targets, in this play, of O'Casey's typical, heavily-biased scorn. But a deeper anger can be felt running through it, directed against poverty, misery and all meanness of spirit. Yet it is worth noticing how much irony is mixed with the anger. O'Casey no more paints his characters in simple black and white than he depicts a situation which is wholly tragic or wholly comic. The Doctor, for example, may appear as the somewhat Dickensian 'villain' of the piece, but some of his remarks at the end show him to be not so much a heartless man as an impatient one, driven to exasperation by overwork and hopeless conditions. Red Muffler is in a way the play's 'hero', a potential rebel, but he acts indecisively and ineffectually. The patients, as a group, are stupid, ignorant and gullible as well as funny and sad and warmly human. For however much O'Casey may sympathize with the poor, he blames them roundly for being spineless and defeatist. 'Yous are afraid to fight these things', Red Muffler cries out, 'That's what's th' matther—we're all afraid to fight.'

# HALL OF HEALING

*The waiting-room of the Parish Dispensary in Dublin,
on a winter's day. It is a place where the poor, sick, or
diseased are looked at and, usually, rewarded with a
bottle. It is an ugly room, drab, and not too clean. The
few bright spots in it are the posters warning of disease.
Running along the back wall is a bench on which the
patients sit while waiting to go in to the Doctor. A
shorter bench runs along the wall to the left. Beyond
this bench is the entrance door which leads from the
waiting-room to the hall, and thence into the street. In
the centre of the back wall is a window which looks out
into the street. Just to the right of this window, a
wooden partition comes down, somewhat diagonally,
through nearly two-thirds of the room, and then turns
to the right, till it is joined to the side wall on the right.
Within this partitioned part of the room are the Surgery
and the Dispensary. A door in this partition wall, up
towards the back, admits one to the Surgery. Another
door in that part of the partition which has turned to
the right, near the right side wall, gives entry to the
Dispensary. To the left of this door is a small window
(shuttered for the moment), with a narrow ledge in front
of it, through which the remedies are handed out to the
patients. On the back wall, to the left of the window is
a poster on which are the words in black print,* DIPH-
THERIA: BEWARE! *Above the Dispensary window is
another one on which are the words in red,* TUBER-
CULOSIS: BEWARE! *The Caretaker, Aloysius, nicknamed
Alleluia, is fixing a third one, to the right of the window
at back, on which are the words in green,* CANCER:

24

BEWARE! *Through the window [at back] it can be seen that the weather is bad; hurrying flakes of snow are falling in a zigzag way because of the cold wind blowing. At times through the scene, quick and thick flurries of snow pass by the windows outside.*

*The patients are all of one patch, immersed in the same uncertainty and want. The lines of care and weariness on their countenances are the same, save that there are more on the face of the old than on the face of the young. The complexion of the younger is starkly pale; that of Jentree a lemon-yellow; that of the Old Woman, a yellowish-brown; that of Alleluia is pale, with a dot of yellow on the points of the cheeks; that of the Doctor a purplish-white; of the Apothecary a pale one, with a bare hint of struggling ruddiness through the paleness. Though differing in cast of countenance, shape and colour of clothing, they all carry in their faces the lines of conscious, or semi-conscious, uncertainty and resignation.*

*The face of Aloysius is a rather foolish one; his head is narrow at the top, developing down and out to form a square for a chin. His grey eyebrows gather into turned-up tufts at the corners; his tough nose tilts and, though he has no moustache, a grey spade bread grows naturally, or has been trained, into a tilting tuft too. His mouth is wide, inclined to grin, and is always slightly agape. Whenever he moves across the room, he does so in a movement, half run, half glide, as if he skated on a surface fit only to glide over in places. As he glides he bends his body over and forward, as a stiff backed bird might do, holding out his arms from his body as he glides and runs along.*

*Next to the Doctor (to whom he is subservient and of whom he is very much afraid), he is Lord of the Dispen-*

25

*sary, dictating to the out-patients, and making things uncomfortable for them; though they try to please him, and follow his humours as well as they can. He wears a uniform of dark blue, the frock-coat reaching to below his knees. It is ornamented with silver buttons. His trousers are a bit short, coming only to the tops of his boots. His head is covered with a blue-peaked cap, having a wide top, and a narrow strap running along the butt of the peak is fastened on either side by a small silver button. A fussy old fool. He takes off his coat to tackle the job of tacking up the poster. He takes up a hammer, spreads out the poster, and with some difficulty hammers in a tack in one corner. Fixing the opposite one, he drops the tack, and curses, immediately ejaculating, 'Mea culpa, mea culpa'. He fixes that corner, and, in driving the third tack home, he hits his thumb, exclaims with pain, flings down the hammer, and thrusts the injured thumb under his armpit, first giving vent to a yell of agony.*

ALLELUIA (*pacing about the room, and nursing the injured thumb*): Ooh! Sacred Heart! Me thumb's destroyed! May th' curse o'—— (*He checks the profanation by trying to sing in a woeful way*) She's me lady love, she is me baby love. Oooh! (*He again yells in agony, and bends double to squeeze the injured member tighter under his armpit.*) Curse o'——(*He checks himself.*) Oh, Holy St. Harmoniumagnus, succour me! (*He sings woefully again*) I know she likes me, I know she likes me, Because she says so—St. Serenium, ayse th' pain; ayse it, ayse th' agony! Preserve me from pain! Today, tomorrow, an' forever afther! Right on th' tenderest part!

*He goes moaning into the Dispensary, and the clank*

*of bottles is heard. Presently, the door leading into the
Dispensary waiting-room from the street is cautiously
opened, and the shawled head of an* OLD WOMAN *peers
into the room. Then the door is slowly opened, and
the* WOMAN *enters. Her back is bent. Her boots are
broken, and the skirt she wears is old and tattered at
the hem. Shawl, skirt, boots, and all, are mud-coloured.
She shivers and shudders as she comes in, slowly rubbing
her gnarled hands to promote circulation. She goes over
to the bench, and sits down stiffly. She coughs, and then
wipes her mouth with the corner of her shawl. The
clanking of the bottles stops. She gives another
asthmatic cough. and again wipes her mouth with the
end of her shawl. The shutter of the Dispensary window
is pushed up, and* ALLELUIA's *head is thrust out; it looks
round the room, and spies the* OLD WOMAN *sitting on the
bench. The head is withdrawn, the shutter pulled down,
and* ALLELUIA *comes out of the Dispensary, wearing a
bandage round the stricken thumb. He goes over with a
glide to the* WOMAN, *catches her by the arm, pulls her
from the seat, and guides her to the door.*

OLD WOMAN (*protesting feebly, but submitting calmly to
ejection as one to whom it is a familiar part of life*): Ah,
now, Mr. Aloysius, it's only a bare few minutes from the
time of openin'. 'Clare to God, Alleluia, th' weather outside ud perish a body; an' I have within me oul' body a
whole kingdom of aches an' pains!

*Without a word* ALLELUIA *opens room door and leads her
out, a look of determined indignation on his face; they
can be heard going down the hall. Shortly after, he
returns, and shuts the door. He cautiously completes the
hanging up of the poster on the wall. He puts on his
coat. Then he hurries into the Dispensary, comes out*

27

*again with a sweeping-brush, and slides it over the floor,
pushing whatever may be before it under the bench.
While he sweeps, he sings softly, in the rather cracked
voice of an old man, the chorus of 'The Rose of Tralee',
pausing sometimes, as he pushes the brush, to do a bit
of a waltz with it, and picking the song up again from
where he left off, when its resumption seems convenient.*

ALLELUIA (*singing*): She was lovellee an' fayer as ay...
rosebud of summer;
But it wasn't her beautay aylone...that...won me;
Aah, no; 'twas they truth in her...eyes...ever beamin',
That med my lovev Mary...they rose of...Thraa...
lee!

*Nearing the end of the chorus, he is near the door of the
Dispensary, and doing a kind of dancing swirl right
around, as he sings the last line, he glides into the Dispensary and closes the door behind him. After a
moment or two, the entrance door opens and* RED
MUFFLER, *a young man of twenty-five, enters the room.
He looks thin and a little careworn. He is very poorly
and thinly dressed; his muddy-black trousers are
patched with black cloth on one knee. His neck is pro-
tected by a thin, red woollen muffler, and a dark tweed
cap, dotted with snowflakes, is pulled low down over
his eyes. He looks poor, cold, and miserable; but there
seems to be some element of grit in his standing. He
takes his cap off and, holding it by the peak, whirls it
round to shake the heavier dampness from it; then he
replaces it on his head. Between each forefinger and
thumb, he pinches together each leg of his trousers, and
flicks them in an effort to make them feel drier. The*
OLD WOMAN's *head appears round the edge of the door,
peering nervously into the room.* RED MUFFLER *sees her.*

RED MUFFLER (*to* OLD WOMAN): Come in, old lady; here is more shelthered than th' hall, an' a heaven from th' sthreet.

OLD WOMAN (*deprecatingly*): I'll do lovely here. If himself seen me, it's out into th' sthreet I'd go again, an' a body pushin' hard to eighty years isn't proof against th' chill o' th' sleet, an' th' chatther of th' interferin' wind outside.

RED MUFFLER (*irritated by her timidity*): Aw, come in, woman, for God's sake! It's this fear of offendin' that keeps us all so far from th' spice of comfort.

OLD WOMAN (*timidly crossing the threshold*): I wondher if I ought to venthure it? Alleluia 'ill only be shovin' me out again. (*She crosses herself.*) He's a good Catholic, an' maybe he won't now.

RED MUFFLER (*decisively*): Aw, go and sit down, woman. I'll know how to deal with this Alleluia of yours when he shows himself.

OLD WOMAN (*wandering over to the bench*): Th' docthor before this one gave us a bad habit, always leavin' ordhers to let us in before openin' time, if th' weather was grim, or rain was fallin', or even when the sun happened to be too boistherous.

RED MUFFLER: An' what's wrong with th' present docthor?

OLD WOMAN: Aw, he's one o' th' surly specimens. (*She rises stiffly, bending double, and groaning, to come close to him.*) He's partial to th' dhrop. He has th' life frightened outa poor oul' Alleluia. (*She whispers*) He can't abide you to come on Mondays, because of his feelin' frightful afther Sunday's rest.

RED MUFFLER: Why do you come on Monday, then?

OLD WOMAN: It's me one free day. I have to work on all the others.

RED MUFFLER: Is he doin' yeh anny good?

OLD WOMAN: Aw, divil a good, so far; but I'm always hopeful he may.

RED MUFFLER: An' is he hopeful?

OLD WOMAN: Divil a hopeful. He just says I'm wastin' his time comin' here; that me back'll never straighten, an' th' ache'll never end. But you can never tell with God.

RED MUFFLER (*clapping his cold hands against his sides*): An' how much d'ye make outa your work?

OLD WOMAN: A shillin' a day, son; five shillin's a week.

RED MUFFLER: Jasus, that's not much!

OLD WOMAN: It's something, son. You see, I can do only rough an' heavy work now. Me oul' hands is too shaky for any fancy job. I don't need much. I won't worry if only I can outlast life workin'. (*Anxiously*) D'ye know, I don't really think I ought to stay here—a few more slaps from the flauntin' wind, an' one more scattherin' of rain over me can't do me much harm.

RED MUFFLER (*ignoring her anxiety*): An' have you no-one to fight for you; no childhren to stand up for you?

OLD WOMAN: Fight, is it? Fightin' only makes things worse. Of course, I've children, but all married, an' hard set themselves to live. There's one blessin'—I can offer everything up to God.

RED MUFFLER (*venomously*): Misery isn't much of a gift to give to God, is it?

OLD WOMAN (*shocked and staring—after a pause*): Ah, son, don't say a thing like that! We're too poor to take th' risk of sayin' serious things. We're told God is good, an' we need every little help we can get.

RED MUFFLER: An' th' kind docthor before this fellow come—where did he go?

OLD WOMAN: Aw, he went into his grave. Cancer, I'm told. With th' aid o' dhrugs, he kept himself goin' for a year an' a day; then, he was silently seen no more.

RED MUFFLER (*echoing her*): Silently seen no more! Will this damned doctor never come! Such as us have barely time to glimpse a gleam that's kind before it hurries to the dark again. It's afther ten, and that damned docther isn't here;

OLD WOMAN (*anxiously*): Why, aren't you feelin' well, son?

RED MUFFLER: Me? Oh, I'm all right. It's our little girl o' nine: our first one. She's been bad a week; she's worse; now, we're afraid she'll soon be something silently seen no more. (*Tensely*) The child is bad; th' child is worse; th' child is chokin'. (*Agonizingly*) Jesus Christ, ha' mercy!

OLD WOMAN (*soothingly*): I wouldn't be fancyin' death for your little one, son. She'll be all right. God is good. They tell us that God's thought is roomy with anxiety for the very young.

RED MUFFLER (*impatiently*): I know what they tell us, I know, woman; but it's past ten; an' ten's th' hour, an' th' blighter should be here. (*The organ is heard playing.*) What music is that?

OLD WOMAN: An organ in the church next door; every Monday someone plays it: practisin', maybe. When th' wind's this way, you can hear it. The caretaker here dances like a fool, and chants an Alleluia ditty whenever it sounds. That's why we call him Alleluia. (*She comes nearer.*) An oul' fool!

RED MUFFLER: Me feet's numb. It's not good to be left standin' here in these wet things. I'm seepin'.

OLD WOMAN: When you're my age, son, you'll be well used to them things.

*He stamps his feet heavily on the floor in an effort to give them the feel of life. The shutter on window in Dispensary is suddenly pulled up, and the head of* ALLELUIA,

31

*cap and all, is thrust through it. The head peers around
to see who has made the noise, sees* RED MUFFLER, *and
the head is pulled in again, while the shutter is pulled
down with a snap. Then the door of the Dispensary is
opened, and* ALLELUIA *slides out and over to the* RED
MUFFLER. *He takes him by the arm and tries to guide
him to the entrance door, but he is resisted, and* RED
MUFFLER *doesn't budge.*

RED MUFFLER (*shaking off* ALLELUIA'S *hold*): Here, you—
what's bitin' you?

ALLELUIA (*a little taken aback by the unexpected resistance*):
You can't stay here. No one's to cross the sthreet door
till th' regulation time o' openin'. (*He snatches* RED
MUFFLER *by the arm again.*) Come on, now—out!

RED MUFFLER (*violently shaking off* ALLELUIA'S *hold*):
G'way, you fussy fiddlin' fool!

*A little frightened, and deciding that discretion is
needed,* ALLELUIA *side-steps from* RED MUFFLER, *spots the*
OLD WOMAN—*now cowering in a corner—and glides over
to where she sits. He catches her arm; she obediently
rises, and he begins to guide her over to the entrance.*

OLD WOMAN (*timidly apologetic*): I musta strayed in be
mistake, Mister Alleluia—I mean, Mr. Aloysius. Th'
sleet an' the bullyin' wind has made th' sthreet unkind,
sir. Yes, th' wind must ha' blew me in, mister. Without
me noticin' either. You'll excuse me, sir; for I've many
burdens of aches an' pains to try to hide from th' blowin'
blight of th' weather.

ALLELUIA (*decisively*): Yeh can't hide your aches an' pains
here, ma'am. You can't expect to have Alleluia hours of
comfort at your time o' life, or in your circumstances.
Th' last docthor near ruined yous all, so he did, with his
scorn of regulations; with his 'make the bareness

brighter', an' his 'th' most o' them won't last a lot
longer'. Had he lived, he'd ha' wanted cushions for
your poor backsides. Th' waste of it! I'd like to know
how we'd fare without th' regulations.

OLD WOMAN (*meditatively*): Th' last one always had a win-
some word for th' sick an' dyin', so he had.

ALLELUIA: Because he was sick an' dyin' himself—that's
why. Out you go, an' don't put your nose in again, till
th' docthor arrives.

OLD WOMAN (*half turning to glance at* RED MUFFLER): Th'
gentleman behind us, sir, advised me to shelter in outa
th' weather.

ALLELUIA (*pushing her out by the door*): Out you go!

*During all this* RED MUFFLER *has taken no notice, making
no effort to defend the* OLD WOMAN; *but has turned his
back on the other two, and is now staring hard at one of
the posters.*

OLD WOMAN (*reaching the door, hesitates, turns suddenly
round, and runs across the room till she is half-way to
where* RED MUFFLER *is standing—bitterly*): You went
before me when I was comin' in, but you're not before
me goin' out! You keep your courage secret, you do.
(*She makes the motion and the sound of spitting scornfully towards him*) That's your value to this poor oul'
woman, you poor morsel of a man! (ALLELUIA *has now
got behind her with a movement that is half a run,
half a glide, and hastens to shoo her out as a drover
might a cow, adding an occasional shove with his hand
to her back. As she nears the entrance door—fervently*)
Thanks be to God who spared th' last poor docthor be
givin' him death, an' deliverin' him from th' lousy lot
of us!

*She disappears out by the door,* ALLELUIA *following close on her heels.* RED MUFFLER *turns slowly away from the poster, and sinks down to sit on the bench, resting with his elbow on knee, his head on his hand. After a pause, the* DOCTOR *whirls into the room, fussier even than old* ALLELUIA, *followed meekly by the caretaker. The* DOCTOR *is of middle height, rather plump, and widening perceptibly around the belly. His face—half concealed now by a thick white wool muffler—is turning to a purplish tinge by hard drinking. His eyes are small and hard, his eyebrows thick and shaggy. Had he his black bowler hat off, it could be seen that he is bald, save for a few reddish-grey hairs brushed over the crown, in an effort, maybe, to hide a big expanse of polished skull. He is wearing a heavy brown topcoat; and his lower legs are encased in shining black leather leggings; a serviceable umbrella is in his left hand, a satchel in his right one. As he enters, he gives a sudden belch, and he ejaculates, as if to himself, but quite audibly. 'Jasus!' He catches sight of* RED MUFFLER, *and turns to* ALLELUIA.

DOCTOR: Who's that fella? What's that fella doin'?

ALLELUIA: He's waitin' for you, sir.

DOCTOR: An' how'd he get in before the regulation time?

ALLELUIA: He just came in without by your leave from a soul. I expostulated with him, but he wouldn't budge for no-one. Wouldn't budge an inch.

DOCTOR: Then th' street door must have been open to let him in.

ALLELUIA (*sliding to the left and to the right of the Doctor, and back again*): I left it open, sir, for a spessesscific purpose.

DOCTOR: For a what? What d'ye mean, man?

ALLELUIA (*again sliding to right and left, and around, the* DOCTOR *so that the* DOCTOR *has to turn to follow what he's*

*saying*): For you, sir; I didn't want you to be fouled with
the weather an' you fussin' with th' key for th' keyhole.

DOCTOR (*impatiently*): Stop that buzzing round me; you
make me giddy, man. I'm quite competent to find the
keyhole without a fuss. Don't leave that door open again
till the regulation time. If I've forgotten the key, I can
ring, can't I? (*As* ALLELUIA *is silent*) Damn it, I can ring,
can't I?

ALLELUIA: Yis, yis; of course you can ring; 'course you can,
sir.

DOCTOR: And you're not deaf, man, as well as bothered,
are you?

ALLELUIA: Me deaf? (*With a dancing glide before the*
DOCTOR) I'd hear the cuckoo before it came, sir.

DOCTOR: Well, hear the surgery bell when it rings, for I'm
not in a waiting mood today. How many are outside,
d'ye know?

ALLELUIA: I seen six or seven or eight, or maybe nine, when
I peeped into the street.

DOCTOR (*sarcastically*): Are you sure it wasn't ten, now?

ALLELUIA: It might ha' well been ten, for the sleet was
fallin' between me an' them. More than ten, maybe, sir.

DOCTOR: Well, you can get them in, and, mind you, no
delay when the bell rings. Immediately one enthers, pop
another at the edge of the surgery door to be ready
when the bell sounds again.

ALLELUIA (*doing another gliding dance to the right, to the
left of the* DOCTOR): On their tiptoes; ears cocked; tense
with listenin', prepared to spring forward when they
hear a tinkle.

DOCTOR (*thrusting the umbrella under his right arm, and
gripping the shoulder of* ALLELUIA *with his left hand,
which he uses to give him a shake*): Keep still you rub-
bered image of desolation! When the bell gives two

35

quick rings, it's you I want, not a patient. And listen: no gossiping while you're on duty—d'ye hear?

ALLELUIA: Gossip, is it? Me gossip? An' on duty? Aw, never! The' only words I ever uses is expended on expostulations. Never fear, sir; I keep well within th' silences of devotion. Gossip on duty is not good company.

DOCTOR (*explosively*): Aren't you always at it! Expostulations! Give your expostulations a rest today, and just shove them in to me.

ALLELUIA: You don't know them, doctor; if you did, you wouldn't wondher any. Not a one o' them'll budge without an expostulation.

DOCTOR (*wildly*): Looka here, if you don't learn to quit yourself better than you do, I'll complain to the Guardians, by God, I will! (*He gives a more violent and sickly belch.*) Ooh, damn it! You're making me worse! If you have me yelling at you today, it'll be th' worse for you. Have you th' Surgery fire going well?

ALLELUIA (*cheerfully—and beginning to slide about again*): Yissir; oh, ay: it's a beauty; all aglow, an' most enticin'. I'd hurry in to it, an' get them damp things off you.

DOCTOR: They're not damp! (*Near a shout*) I came in a cab!

ALLELUIA: An' a wise man you were, doctor, to do it.

DOCTOR (*impatiently*): Get them in, man, and get them out! No dallying today.

*He hurries towards the Surgery;* RED MUFFLER *rises again from the bench to meet him.* ALLELUIA *hurries out by the entrance door, and soon returns followed by the patients, sorry-looking men and women from the tenements.* ALLELUIA *stands at the entrance door ushering them in, and waving them to the benches. As they troop in, the organ is heard playing again, and the poor patients seem to fall in with the rhythm of the tune as they drag themselves to the benches.*

*Among them are* BLACK MUFFLER; *the old bent-back woman; a Young Woman of twenty-three, who, behind her hand, gives an occasional dry, hard cough;* MR. JENTREE, *a man of forty-five, dressed in a mode of faded respectability—bowler hat, black, somewhat discoloured; faded brown tweed coat, waistcoat, and trousers; stiff white collar and black tie; and a brown mackintosh. As he enters, his head is shaking, a strained look of anxiety disturbs his face which is fortified by a short beard and moustache. He walks uncertainly with the aid of a stick. He sits down between the* YOUNG WOMAN *and the* OLD WOMAN. *While seated, first his right leg, and then his left one, gives a sudden and spasmodic jerk, signifying a nervous disorder. Among them is* GREEN MUFFLER, *a man of about thirty-five, clad in the rough clothes of a labourer—corduroy trousers, old khaki coat from the remains of the first world war, thick coat of a faded dark blue, and a green muffler round his neck. When he enters, he looks nervously around him, as if asking himself if it were well for him to be there. And when he sits down on the last bit of bench, he stretches his head forward to look at the posters. The other patients are but variants of the others in feature and colour of clothing.*

RED MUFFLER (*going in front of the* DOCTOR *before he gets to the Surgery door*): Excuse me, sir; I want to ask you about our kid.

DOCTOR (*brusquely*): What kid? Sit down, sit down, man, and take your turn.

RED MUFFLER: I'm not ill meself, sir; I've only come about our little girl who's very bad.

DOCTOR (*impatiently*): Sit down, sit down, till I'm ready for you.

RED MUFFLER (*speaking rapidly for fear the* DOCTOR *would get away*): You seen her a week ago, sir. She's worse, an' th' missus's afraid for her.

DOCTOR (*sharply and rapidly*): Oh, sit down when you're told, man!

RED MUFFLER (*submissively complying*): Yessir.

*The* DOCTOR *hurries into the Surgery.* ALLELUIA *obsequiously closes door after him.* RED MUFFLER *resumes his seat nervously, pulling his coat round him; buttoning it up, and then opening it again.*

YOUNG WOMAN (*coughing behind her hand*): He's in a bad mood today.

OLD WOMAN: When's he any other way? Since the last doctor's death th' last light left us has gone out.

BLACK MUFFLER (*morosely*): What odds? Th' fella taken away done no more for us than this fella that's left. It's a new doctor, but it's th' old, old treatment. I dunno that th' last one was fit to be a docthor at all.

OLD WOMAN (*scornfully*): You dunno! Who're you to dunno? Why wasn't he fit?

BLACK MUFFLER: Well, ma'am, th' last time he saw me, he said what I needed was betther food, a finer house to live in, an' a lot more enjoyment. An' when I said couldn't you give me a bottle, docthor, he laughed at me, so that I felt ashamed of me life. An' afther what he had said, d'ye know what he said then?

JENTREE (*impatiently*): Then what did he say, what did he say, then?

BLACK MUFFLER: My good young man, he said, you can't expect to dhrink health into you out of a bottle. Nobody knows how frightened I felt!

YOUNG WOMAN: Wouldn't any sensible one be frightened at th' edge on a remark like that!

OLD WOMAN: Poor innocent man—no wondher th' good God took him to Himself!

BLACK MUFFLER: When he saw th' fright I was in, he put a hand on me shouldher, and said, Looka, says he, if health could be got out of a bottle, says he, I'd be th' healthiest man alive. An' me heart galloped into th' fear that th' poor man wasn't a docthor at all! Unless he was beginnin' to go out of his mind. I've never been th' same since.

JENTREE: I dunno how life could be lived without some kinda bottles.

OLD WOMAN: What if th' poor man did make a slip aself— it's a wise man doesn't. He just had some kind of a kink against bottles.


*Meanwhile, ALLELUIA has gone into the Dispensary, and returns with a stick of chalk. With this he draws a straight line on the floor, half-way between the bench and the Surgery door. Just outside this door, draws a circle. Within the circle, he puts a patient facing the door, and places another patient toeing the line, facing, too, towards the Surgery door. The Surgery bell rings. ALLELUIA hurries the patient in the circle into the Surgery, shoves the other patient into it, while another one toes the line. When the first patient comes out, she goes to the Dispensary, hands in a bottle, gets it back full, and then she goes away by the entrance door, shivering with anticipation at what she will meet out-side. This goes on rapidly till a stream of patients have passed in, come out, and gone away. ALLELUIA hurries each in when the bell tinkles, hurries each to the Dis-pensary window for the medicine, and then hurries each out of the place. This is the common measure of the place, and it goes on rapidly till* BLACK MUFFLER *passes from the line to the circle, and from the circle into the Surgery. As each poor patient comes out to go away,* ALLELUIA *waylays him or her, holding a card out to them, and asking a penny for the Holy Souls, that Masses may be said for their redemption from Purgatory. When he gets a penny, he pricks a space in the card he holds in his hand with a pin. The organ is heard playing the same tune during the procession of patients, and* ALLELUIA *goes about in a dancing slide to the tune, chanting mockingly,* 'ALLELUIA, ALLELUIA, ALLELUIA', *waylaying the patients for pennies at intervals, challenging them with the phrase 'Remember the Holy Souls in Purgatory'.* BLACK MUFFLER *comes out of the Surgery cautiously and softly shuts the door behind him.*

BLACK MUFFLER (*gesturing back towards the Surgery with his thumb—in a whisper*): Hunted me out! Lyin' down on a couch, with th' Dispenser givin' him a cordial. Looks like a cut-down daisy. We'll be here all day.

YOUNG WOMAN: Maybe it'll give time for the weather to clear.

ALLELUIA *glides down the room, bends down, hands on knees, before* GREEN MUFFLER, *and stares at him. The patients watch the glide, and* BLACK MUFFLER—*again in the circle—and the rest— except* JENTREE—*turn to watch and listen.*

ALLELUIA (*to* GREEN MUFFLER): You're a new customer here, aren't you?

GREEN MUFFLER (*staring back at him*): I was never here before, if that's what you mean.

ALLELUIA: An' what are you complainin' of, me man?

GREEN MUFFLER: Eh? (*Stretching out his right arm carefully and slowly*) Oh, just this arm o' mine—it hurts terrible when I thry to do anything serious.

ALLELUIA: Aah, rheumatism!

GREEN MUFFLER (*shortly*): Naw, it's not rheumatism! I know what rheumatism is.

ALLELUIA (*thoughtfully*): It might be something goin' against th' blood strame.

GREEN MUFFLER (*with sharpness and mockery*): Are you th' doctor, or wha'?

ALLELUIA (*importantly*): I'm the next to th' doctor. Where's your bottles?

GREEN MUFFLER (*somewhat startled*): Bottles? What bottles?

ALLELUIA: There's no use o' you comin' here if you're not thoughtfully and thoroughly supplied with bottles. Every commencer must have three—one for a draught, one for a liniment, and one for a mixture. You can't go into the doctor's presence unless you are in possession of three comely and commodious bottles.

GREEN MUFFLER (*impressed*): I didn't know nothin' about bottles.

OLD WOMAN (*leaning forward as far as she can from the bench towards* GREEN MUFFLER): You might need only one, son; but th' nature of your particular throuble might require two; an' in a diversified complaint, three bottles might be called for; so you have to be prepared. Stands to reason, a patient must be provided with a bottle, or two, or three bottles. As likely as not, son, you'll be a three-bottle man.

*The patients are now more interested than ever in the discussion; the one in the circle of chalk moves out of it to be nearer; and the one toeing the line moves nearer too.* JENTREE *is the only one who is occupied with himself, and takes no notice.*

ALLELUIA (*not liking the interference—turning towards the* OLD WOMAN, *with his body still bent double and hands on knees*): If you'll allow me, ma'am, I'd have you notice that this would-be patient is receivin' official attention an' insthruction respectin' any bottles necessary in combination with his ailment.

YOUNG WOMAN (*coughing behind her hand*): One ud never never know, be th' common look of them, that bottles was so important. With every patient, bottles there must be!

BLACK MUFFLER: Bottles there was, bottles there is, bottles there must be!

ALLELUIA (*angrily—to the patients in general*): Are yous goin' to have me expostulatin' all th' day! Close your gobs, an' cease from shattherin' me explanations to this man!

GREEN MUFFLER: Th' whole place seems to be seethin' with bottles. An' where am I goin' to get them?

*The Surgery bell has been signalling for* ALLELUIA—*by giving two quick, consecutive rings—several times; but all are so excited over, and interested in, the bottles that no-one takes the slightest notice.*

OLD WOMAN (*over to* GREEN MUFFLER): If you've thruppence on you, son, you'll get them in some pub: black porther or green mineral bottles—it doesn't matter, for they're all good of their kind.

ALLELUIA (*accompanying* GREEN MUFFLER *out by the entrance*): An' remember, they must be all rinsed clean so as to be in a receptionable condition for th' contention of medicine.

*The bell sounds its two quick, consecutive rings again, this time with venomous clarity in the now silent room, startling the patients back into meek and anxious attention.*

YOUNG WOMAN (*agitated*): Holy Saint Juniper o' Judea, there's th' docthor callin' a patient!

OLD WOMAN (*to the patient who has been standing in the chalk circle—vigorously*): Off you go; in with you!

BLACK MUFFLER (*bewildered by the sudden change of topic*): Who? Is it me, is it?

OLD WOMAN (*rapidly*): You, you; yes, you. Hop it, man!

YOUNG WOMAN (*beginning before the* OLD WOMAN *ends*): Quick. Yes, you!

JENTREE (*beginning before the* YOUNG WOMAN *ends*): Before he's out on top of us, roarin'!

BLACK MUFFLER *makes a bewildered rush for the Surgery door which he opens. He goes in, but immediately comes out again, pushed back by the* DOCTOR, *who is angry and furious.*

DOCTOR (*wildly*): Not you, not you! Aloysius I rang for! Good God, that fellow'll drive me mad! (*Shouting*) Aloysius!

ALLELUIA (*sliding into the room again—full of hurry and fear*): Sir, sir; here, sir!

DOCTOR (*stormily*): Where were you, you dolt! Didn't you here the bell? You'll quit this very week-end! What were you doing, you deaf oul' ditherer?

ALLELUIA (*rapidly*): Explainin' regulations to a patient, sir, about bottles.

DOCTOR (*furious*): You fool, what do bottles matter! My pen—where is it? Pen, pen, man!

ALLELUIA (*flustered, but smiling*): Pen? Oh, the pen, is it?

43

Oh, yes, the pen. Let me think, now. I remember, yes; th' apothecary got a loan of it, sir.

DOCTOR (*angrily*): Get it back then, at once. He's no business to touch it! Let him get a pen of his own. This is th' third or fourth time he's pinched it!

ALLELUIA (*deprecatingly*): Not pinched, sir; oh, no, not pinched it.

DOCTOR (*roaring*): Pinched, I say! (*He gives a half-belch ending in a sigh—ejaculating as if to himself*) Oh, God, I'm in a shockin' state! (*To* ALLELUIA—*angrily*) Why th' hell d'ye let him take it?

ALLELUIA (*whisperingly*): Between ourselves, sir. I'm tired expostulatin' with him. You'd want to chain it to your desk, sir.

DOCTOR: Wish I could chain you where you'd be hidden from view! (*Pushing* ALLELUIA *from him*) Go, an' get th' pen! (*To* RED MUFFLER, *who has risen, and now takes a step towards him*) Oh, sit down, you; sit down!

*Crestfallen,* RED MUFFLER *does so. The Apothecary's head is poked out of the Dispensary window; the head is completely bald, except for a tiny web of fringe above the forehead; a thick moustache covers the upper lip, and almost hides the mouth; it juts out aggressively at each side of the face. The head twists round in the direction of the voices.*

APOTHECARY'S HEAD (*shouting*): Aloysius; eh, Aloysius!

ALLELUIA (*running round to the window*): Yessir.

APOTHECARY'S HEAD (*thrusting out an arm holding a pen*): Here's th' damned pen for him!

ALLELUIA *snatches the pen, and rushes back to the* DOCTOR, *who snatches it from him.*

DOCTOR (*indicating with his pen* BLACK MUFFLER *who had stood within the chalk circle*): You there—come in.

44

Come on, come on!

*He goes into the Surgery.*

ALLELUIA (*fussy as ever—getting behind the patient, and pushing him along*): Go on, go on, go on!

GREEN MUFFLER *enters by the entrance door. He is damp and shivery. He carries a porter bottle under an arm, and the neck and shoulders of mineral-water bottles are sticking out from the side pockets of his coat. He sits down, silent and morose, on the end of the bench. ALLELUIA beckons the YOUNG WOMAN, and places her within the chalk circle. He takes another patient from the bench and puts him toeing the line; bending down to shove back a foot that ventures over it, arranging the feet so that they exactly touch the sacred chalk line.*

ALLELUIA (*petulantly fixing the foot*): Keep the feet determined toein' the line exact, will you!

YOUNG WOMAN (*nervously*): I hope I won't be called on to stand too long here—I always feel shaky when I stand for long in th' one place.

OLD WOMAN: He'll take a long time between patients today; always does when he's bad from booze.

JENTREE (*giving a sudden jerk in his seat*): You know, if I don't get some specific attention soon an' sudden, something terrible's bound to happen. I'll fall, paralysed, from me neck down!

OLD WOMAN (*soothingly*): You're lettin' it, whatever it is, play on you too much, son.

JENTREE (*testily*): Aw, for God's sake, woman, talk sense. Can't I feel me legs goin' dead? D'ye imagine I can go on not noticin' things? (*A leg gives a spasmodic jerk.*) Oh! Did yous all see that? (*To* ALLELUIA) Eh, misther, I'll have to be let in at oncst!

ALLELUIA (*with a sweeping glide towards* JENTREE *and a bend-down to place his face in front of* JENTREE'S): You'll wait till th' regulation tinkle of th' bell tells you to go.

JENTREE (*as the other leg gives a spasmodic jerk upwards*): Oh! There, did yous all see that one go up? There's no deception, mind yous—I'm really in a desperate condition!

YOUNG WOMAN (*in the circle*): Poor man! An' what gave you them terrible jerks? What did th' docthor say?

JENTREE (*with scorn*): Th' docthors! Th' one before this one, an' this fella, too, said it was because of too much imbibin' of wine.

OLD WOMAN (*startled*): Wine? An' where would you come across th' quantity of wine to give you them sharp an' sudden jitters?

JENTREE: I was a wine porter, ma'am, but th' little I lowered through th' years couldn't possibly ha' done it.

OLD WOMAN (*realising the cause, but not willing to hurt*): Looka that now. I wouldn't say all; but it might, it only might, mind you, have had a little to do with it.

JENTREE (*getting on to his feet with a shivering jerky movement*): Oh! Th' bottle I get is doin' me damn all of good! An' th' wather I have to dhrink's makin' me worse! Looka, I'm thremblin' all over!

OLD WOMAN (*to the other patients who are now all interested in* JENTREE): His mind's sthrayin'. (*To* JENTREE) Wather? What wather are you dhrinkin', son?

JENTREE (*venomously*): Th' wather them getts o' docthors ordhered me to lower—more'n half a gallon a day. (*He sinks back onto the bench.*) Me left leg's lost its motion. Not in a year, mind you, but in a day! I'd like to see him thryin' it himself. (*He jerks up from the bench again.*) I'll have to be carried home, if this goes on!

What manner o' mortal man could swally a tank of wather in a single day?

OLD WOMAN: Indeed, son, th' boyo inside wouldn't like to have to do it himself.

JENTREE: I feel close to death when I see the sight of it!

OLD WOMAN: Th' sight of what, son?

JENTREE (*explosively*): Wather, woman; th' wather!

ALLELUIA (*coming close to the talkers*): There's only one thing, ma'am, manifested enough to negify th' effects o' wine, an' that's wather; an' th' patient would be well advised to gulp it down, gulp it down with determination, ad lib.

OLD WOMAN (*eagerly—to* JENTREE): Hear that, son? Mr. Aloysius knows what's good for you! Wholesome stuff is wather. Gulp it down, son, an' its bound to negify any wine that may be ripplin' round in you still: ad lib's th' only way!

JENTREE (*to* OLD WOMAN—*determinedly*): I'd have you remember, ma'am, that I'm th' custodian of me own ailments, an' am fully endorsed on their concern and their keepin'! (*Indignantly—to* ALLELUIA) Gulp it down! I wondher would you relish gulpin' cold wather down you till your heart was stunned into stoppin' its beatin'? Would you like to gulp cold wather down you till every vital organ in your poor body was frightened of what was floodin' into them? Negify th' effects o' wine! An' if I go on, what'll I take to negify th' effects of wather?

OLD WOMAN (*to* JENTREE): Sure that's the difficulty son. (*To* ALLELUIA) If th' poor man has to negify th' wine with wather, and then has to negify the wather with wine, sure th' poor man'll burst himself thryin' to find a solution for his ailment.

JENTREE (*to* OLD WOMAN): Sure that's what I'm up against all the time, an' no-one'll listen to me! (*Rising shaking*

to his feet and sitting down again—*a little hysterical*)
What's keepin' that fella inside! I'm goin' fast. Th'
thremors is mountin' me spine. I'll be gone in a minute,
if he doesn't hurry to have a look at me!

YOUNG WOMAN (*from the circle*): Poor man, y'are in a
terrible state! Maybe you'd like to take my turn? I'm
in no hurry, so I'm not. Indeed, I'd rather wait as long
as I can in th' hope th' weather ud be better when I set
out for home.

OLD WOMAN (*to* JENTREE—*encouragingly*): Yes, do; go on,
son; take your chance of an earlier overhaul.

*She rises, and, with the help of the* YOUNG WOMAN—
*coughing with the exertion—planks* JENTREE *in the circle.*
*He is shaky, nervous, and leans heavily on his stick.*
*The* YOUNG *and the* OLD WOMEN *then return, and sit*
*down on the bench. The Surgery door opens gently,*
*and* BLACK MUFFLER *enters the waiting-room on tiptoe,*
*a frightened look on his face. He closes the Surgery*
*door softly, and gives an admonitory and warning ges-*
*ture with a prescription he is holding in a hand.*

BLACK MUFFLER (*with a significant wave of a hand*):
Husssh! He's in a murtherin' mood today! Can't sit aysy
a second. Went out once, an' I heard him thryin' to
retch. He'll take ages to get through today. Jasus, we
poor have a lot to bear!

RED MUFFLER (*rising to his feet—angry and fierce*): An'
why do they bear it! Even with the best docthor in its
bosom, what kind of kip is this place? I deny that this
is all that God has got to give us! Even with the best
music of a church organ, what betther could we do here
but dance a dance of death! I won't do it; I won't do it!
By God, if that fella inside refuses to come to our sick
kid, I'll know th' reason why!

48

*He sinks down on the bench again, wiping his forehead
with a soiled rag he has taken from a pocket. After this
outburst, for a little while, there is a dead silence, the
patients, standing and sitting, staring at the fiercely-
spoken* RED MUFFLER. *Then* BLACK MUFFLER *goes to the
window of the Dispensary, hands in his prescription and
a bottle; waits a moment, then gets the bottle back filled
with a rich yellow fluid. He comes to the middle of the
room, and holds the bottle from him towards the light.*

BLACK MUFFLER (*holding the bottle at arm's length*): Oh, a
lovely yella, this time; th' last was blue.

YOUNG WOMAN: Mine was red, so it was.

OLD WOMAN: Show us. (*He hands her the bottle, and she
holds it out at arm's length.*) So 'tis—gorgeous yella!
(*She hands the bottle back to him.*) Be th' look of it,
son, that should do you a power o' good. This fella
thinks more o' bottles than th' other fella did—I'll say
that of him!

ALLELUIA (*down at the entrance, beckoning* BLACK MUFFLER
*to go*): Eh, you, with the black muffler, there; you've
been fully medicamented, an' you've been handed your
documented mixture; (*he glides up to* BLACK MUFFLER) so
no more chit-chat, but go; but before you go, remember
the Holy Souls.

BLACK MUFFLER (*ignoring* ALLELUIA'S *appeal—pocketing the
bottle*): I'll enther a new lease o' life when I stoke meself
up with this documented stimulant, wha'? I'll renew th'
bottle, he says. Well, we'll thry it once more, anyway.

ALLELUIA *slides and glides up to* BLACK MUFFLER, *catches
him by the arm, and glides down with him to the
entrance door, ushering him out to the street.*

JENTREE (*becoming more nervous*): What's keepin' him;
what's th' fella doin' at all? I'm gettin' worse. I'll be

down prostrate, numb an' nameless, before th' fella lets me in!

OLD WOMAN (*encouragingly*): Keep calm, son. Take your thoughts off yourself.

JENTREE (*turning angrily to* OLD WOMAN): Don't be rattlin' nonsense into me mind, woman, an' me in agony! I need immediate aid to countheract what's comin'. I can't wait. I want help at once; now! (*He totters rapidly over to the Surgery door; kicks it below with a foot, bangs it above with his stick.*) These docthors wouldn't blink an eyelid if a man passed into oblivion! (*He again kicks and hammers on the door.*) Eh, eh, you in there, does medical discretion always go disregarded in this place?

*As* JENTREE *is hammering at the door, it suddenly opens, and the* DOCTOR, *furious with anger, appears.* JENTREE *totters back a little, and the patients sit straight and still with respect and a little fear. The patient toeing the line runs off to sit down demurely on the bench.*

DOCTOR (*in an agony of rage*): What's this, my God, what's all this? (*To* JENTREE) Was it you who hammered at the door?

JENTREE (*smilingly*): Me, sir? I just gave a few quiet knocks, sir, for I was feelin' fit to die.

DOCTOR (*yelling*): Aloysius! Oh, where's that rambling fool! Aloysius!

ALLELUIA *comes rushing in and over to the* DOCTOR. *He grips* JENTREE *and pulls him into the circle again.*

ALLELUIA (*to* JENTREE): Stand there; don't budge!

DOCTOR (*furiously—to* ALLELUIA): I'll budge you, you Poor Law Guardian's gett!

ALLELUIA (*ignoring the* DOCTOR—*pulling the other patient to toe the line again*): Stand there; don't budge!

50

DOCTOR (*talking rapidly, pulling* ALLELUIA *by the coat to a place near the Surgery door*): You stand there, and don't budge till they're all in and out again! (*To* JENTREE) I told you not to come for a month. I gave you enough bromide mixture for a month. You're not going to die. Be off home.

JENTREE: Yessir, nosir. But th' delugin' o' wather y'ord-hered's doin' me no good.

DOCTOR: Take more of it, then, to weaken the wine in you. Now off you go. (*To the* YOUNG WOMAN) You're Jenny Sullivan, aren't you?

YOUNG WOMAN (*with a prologue of a cough*): Yessir.

DOCTOR (*to* OLD WOMAN): What do you want—more liniment?

OLD WOMAN: Yessir, please.

DOCTOR: Get it then, and go. (*Indicating* GREEN MUFFLER) Who's that man?

ALLELUIA (*sliding into a bending position before the* DOCTOR): A three-bottle man; a newcomer.

DOCTOR (*calling down to him*): Eh, you, come on in to me.

*He returns to the Surgery.*

JENTREE (*as he goes out*): Weaken th' wine in me! It's in an ambulance I ought to be, speedin' to a place where a qualified man ud be sacked if he left me out of his sight for a minute! I'll appeal to the authorities, so I will—this very day!

OLD WOMAN: Arra, be sensible, son! Let what they give kill or cure us, there's ne'er a one for us to appeal to, bar the good God Himself! The poor who refuse to be patient, die young.

RED MUFFLER (*fiercely*): We've been too patient too long; too damned long; too god-damned long, I'm sayin'! Patience is only th' holy name for suicide!

51

ALLELUIA *glides along with* GREEN MUFFLER *to the Surgery door, ushers him in, and is about to close the door when the* DOCTOR *gives him a note.*

DOCTOR: Give that to Jenny Sullivan there, and tell her she can go.

ALLELUIA *gives the* YOUNG WOMAN *the note. The* OLD WOMAN *has crossed to the Dispensary window, handed in her prescription and bottle; received her liniment, and returned to the back to gaze out of the window at the falling snow.*

OLD WOMAN (*tonelessly*): Th' snowy rain is worse nor what it was even.

YOUNG WOMAN: Looka what I've got; looka what he's given me!

OLD WOMAN: An' what is it, daughter?

YOUNG WOMAN (*tonelessly*): A note to the Consumption Dispensary o' Charles Street. I'm done for now. I feel faint. I'll lose me job an' all, now. It's me death warrant!

OLD WOMAN (*coming over to her*): Sit still for a few minutes, an' then we'll go home together. You'll have a lot more to go through before you'll be done for. There, sit still, child. I wouldn't say that he wasn't mistaken—th' fellow doesn't know black from white this mornin'. An' anyway, daughter, death's th' last thing th' poor should dhread.

*A* LAD *of fifteen years of age comes into the waiting-room, and* ALLELUIA *at once glides down to him. The boy is thinly clad in coat and long trousers too big for him. His cap, too, is a size too large. He has the mask-like paleness of the others.*

ALLELUIA (*to the* LAD): What d'ye want?

LAD (*handing* ALLELUIA *a red ticket*): For me mother for the docthor to call.

ALLELUIA (*reprovingly*): Sir, sir; don't forget th' sir, lad. Are you workin'?

LAD: I deliver th' papers of a mornin'. I get two shillin's a week.

ALLELUIA: An' how much d'ye keep for yourself?

LAD: Fourpence.

ALLELUIA: Sir, sir; don't forget th' sir—where were you brought up? Don't you know your catechism?

LAD: Wha'?

ALLELUIA: Wha'! That's not th' way to addhress a superior. How much o' th' last fourpence have you left?

LAD: Tuppence, sir; only tuppence.

ALLELUIA: Ah, that's better. (*He shows the* LAD *the collecting-card.*) Remember th' Holy Souls. Put one o' th' pennies on th' card for th' Holy Souls.

*After some hesitation, the* LAD *forks out a penny and gives it to* ALLELUIA, *who marks it down by pricking the card with a pin.*

LAD (*earnestly*): Me mother says, sir, she's very sick an' can't stir in th' bed, an' would th' doctor please hurry to her?

ALLELUIA (*almost shoving the* LAD *out*): Tell your mother that th' docthor'll go full gallop to her!

GREEN MUFFLER *now comes from the Surgery and goes to the Dispensary window. He planks his three bottles down on the ledge in front of the hand-out window, and then hands in his prescription to the* APOTHECARY. ALLELUIA *glides over to him, in the hope of collecting another penny for the Holy Souls.*

ALLELUIA (*archly holding collecting card under* GREEN MUFFLER'S *nose*): A penny to help the Holy Souls outa Purgatory, kind man o' th' three big bottles.

APOTHECARY'S VOICE (*at the window—to* GREEN MUFFLER):
Take them bottles away.

ALLELUIA *is startled; lowers card, and listens.*

GREEN MUFFLER (*startled and puzzled*): Eh? Wha'? What
bottles?

APOTHECARY'S VOICE (*impatiently*): Them on th' ledge.
(*Shouting*) Them on th' ledge!

ALLELUIA, *scenting danger, glides away, and stands as
close as he can get to the Surgery door.*

GREEN MUFFLER: I was ordered to bring three bottles. Th'
person in authority here said I must have three bottles
on me. Bring, says he, three bottles, says he, one for a
liniment, one for a mixture, says he, an' one for a
draught.

APOTHECARY'S VOICE (*impatiently*): Do what you're told
man! (*Shouting*) Take them outa the way! They're no
use here!

GREEN MUFFLER *takes the three bottles from the ledge
and deposits them on the floor. After a moment or two,
the* APOTHECARY'S *hand puts a tiny box of pills on the
ledge in front of* GREEN MUFFLER. *He is shocked, looking
at the tiny box, and then at the bottles.*

GREEN MUFFLER (*to the patients—who keep a tense silence*):
Did yous see what's after happenin'? Did yous or did
yous not? Yous all saw me entherin' burdened with
bottles, be strict orders forced to spend me last penny to
get them. An' when I present them, as sthrictly ordered
be a certain person, I'm shouted at to take them away,
an' even th' use of one was denied me. (*He extends his
hand with the tiny pill-box on its palm.*) Looka what I
got! (*He comes into the centre of the room.*) I'm not
dhreamin', mind you. This isn't fairyland either. Yous

all seen what happened. After me huntin' after bottles, looka what's been handed out! (*He glares towards where* ALLELUIA *is busy totting up what he has collected on his card—ostensibly unaware of what is taking place.*) Yous all heard what a certain person said to me. You must have three bottles, he says, one for a mixture, one for a liniment, he says, an' one for a draught. Three, mind you. Yous all sung a song about the necessity for bottles. An' what was the outcome? Yous all seen it yourselves. Yous all see the bottles scattered about, an' me left with what's shinin' in th' palm of me hand! I'm not dhreamin', mind you! Have yous nothin' to say to relieve me feelin's? (*He moves towards the door to go.*) Jasus, it's a cruel thing to do on anyone. (*He turns to look towards the patients.*) An', mind you, that certain person thried to cadge another penny off me for the Holy Souls! An' what about th' sufferin' souls here, eh? (*He goes to the door, and turns again.*) God forbid I'd ever come here again; but if I have to, I warn that certain person not to mention bottles to me; for if that certain person does, he'll be a sufferin' soul in Purgatory himself, without a one to help him out!

*He goes slowly out, leaving the bottles on the floor beside the Dispensary; and, as he goes, he fixes his gaze on the pill-box.*

*The* DOCTOR *comes from the Surgery, dressed for the street as he was when we first saw him. He sees the patients sitting on the bench.*

DOCTOR (*calling*): Aloysius! (ALLELUIA *comes gliding up to him.*) Why are these still there? Why haven't they gone home?

OLD WOMAN (*apologetically—to the* DOCTOR): The Young

Woman here felt faint, an' we were restin' till she got a bit betther.

DOCTOR: She can't rest here. It's nearly closing time. The best place for her is home. (*To* OLD WOMAN) Do you live near her?

OLD WOMAN: Only a sthreet away, sir.

DOCTOR: Well, see her safe home, like a good woman. (*To* ALLELUIA) Close the house up, Aloysius. (*To* RED MUFFLER *who has come close to him*) What is it you want, and speak quick, for I'm in a hurry.

RED MUFFLER: It's me child, sir; me little girl, sir, only just nine years old.

DOCTOR: Yes, yes; what about her?

RED MUFFLER: We're afraid for her. You saw her four days ago; top room, hundhred an' one Hill Sthreet, sir. We want you to come at once.

DOCTOR: I know, I know; everyone wants the doctor to come at once. I'll come sometime tomorrow.

*The* DOCTOR *makes a step forward towards the entrance door, but* RED MUFFLER *makes one too, so that he stands somewhat in the way of the* DOCTOR'S *passage to the door. At the same time, the* APOTHECARY *comes out of the Dispensary. He is dressed for the street—long mackintosh, thick white and red muffler, and a grey trilby hat pulled well down on his forehead. He carries an attaché-case and a walking-stick. He stands outside the Dispensary door and watches what is going on.*

RED MUFFLER (*blocking the* DOCTOR'S *way to the door*): No, today, sir, please: now. She needs you now. Have a look at her, at least. Last night was one of agony to th' missus an' me, listenin' to her losin' her breath. We're afraid soon she'll silently be seen no more. She's bad; she's worse; she's chokin'!

DOCTOR: I'll go tomorrow; I can't go sooner. There are others needing attention, you know.

*He goes to go, but* RED MUFFLER *catches his arm.*

RED MUFFLER (*desperately*): Nine years isn't long enough for a life to live! Damn it, man, if you've none for me, have some thought for th' mother watchin' th' child's rash sthruggles to live!

DOCTOR (*chucking his arm from* RED MUFFLER'S *hold*): Oh, man alive, there are thousands of kids like yours gasping for life in the city today.

RED MUFFLER (*fiercely*): An' no-one seems to care a coloured damn about them!

DOCTOR: No living doctor can give them what they need, man. To worry about them would send me to the grave, too.

*A young woman appears at the entrance door. Her head and half her body are covered by a grey shawl; her thin skirt is black, fading now to a rusty brown; her boots are old, and are sodden with the slush of the streets.*

DOCTOR (*seeing* GREY SHAWL—*angrily to* ALLELUIA): Don't let any more in—put that one out!

ALLELUIA *goes gliding down and tries to turn* GREY SHAWL *back, but she pushes him roughly aside and hastens up to* RED MUFFLER. *The* DOCTOR *is now half-way down to the door;* RED MUFFLER *beside him, a little to his front;* GREY SHAWL *in front of* RED MUFFLER; *the* OLD WOMAN *and the* YOUNG WOMAN *have risen from the bench, and stand behind to the left, almost directly in front of the poster warning of Diphtheria. The* OLD WOMAN *has an arm around the young one, though she needs support herself. The* APOTHECARY *stands a little in front of his Dispensary door.*

RED MUFFLER (*to* GREY SHAWL—*frightened at seeing her*): What'r you doin' here? I had to wait to thry to get th' docthor. Who's with th' child? Why th' hell did you leave her?

GREY SHAWL (*very quietly*): You needn't trouble th' docthor further, Frank. An' I didn't leave little Sheila, it was her who left me.

*Her hand steals forward to cling to a hand of* RED MUFFLER'S, *and there is a silence for some moments.*

RED MUFFLER (*quietly*): Well, we've got all we could get here, so we'd betther go. (*To the* DOCTOR) You might have safely said you'd come, an' kept hope danglin' still in front of us that healin' still was here, an' common goodness. Our little one has had th' charity to save you from a cold an' tirin' journey in th' mornin'. (*Fiercely*) Oh, you blasted fomenter of medicine, you might have listened to what I thried to say!

GREY SHAWL (*frightened*): Frank! Do come home, an' don't make a show of us an' little Sheila. I'm frightened she's feelin' lonely wherever she may be now.

OLD WOMAN (*coaxingly*): Ay, do, son, go home. Ah, it's curious how th' old is left to wither on, while th' young often go before they've time to bloom. It doesn't seem right to me. I could ha' gladly gone in the little one's place; for head down an' back bent, what's for me to thry to tarry here a minute longer! God Almighty does odd things at times.

GREY SHAWL (*coaxingly*): Come on, Frank, till you see her. She's got all her good looks back again. (*Brokenly*) Oh, me little one'll be runnin' round frightened, lookin' for her mammy, among the spirits of the blest!

RED MUFFLER (*to the* DOCTOR): D'ye hear that? She's got

her old good looks all back again. Death has sometimes a kindlier touch than many a human hand.

RED MUFFLER *and* GREY SHAWL *go out followed by the* OLD WOMAN *and the* YOUNG WOMAN, *who pass* RED MUFFLER *and* GREY SHAWL *by as* RED MUFFLER *turns around at the door with a parting shot at the* DOCTOR.

RED MUFFLER (*turning back at the door*): The pair of yous can go home now, an' snore away some other buddin' life! Yous are afraid to fight these things. That's what's th' matther—we're all afraid to fight!

APOTHECARY (*after a pause*): Cheeky boyo, that! Not a grain of gratitude in one of them for all we thry to do for them. Well, I'll be off—good day. It would almost make a man despair of humanity! See you in th' morning.

DOCTOR: Good day. I hope so.

*The* APOTHECARY *goes off.* ALLELUIA *comes gliding down to the* DOCTOR *and holds out the red ticket given to him by the young* LAD.

ALLELUIA (*holding out the ticket*): Another visitin' ticket, sir.

DOCTOR (*impatiently*): Put it on my desk, put it on my desk, man! (ALLELUIA *glides off swiftly, with hand extended holding the red ticket, dives into the Surgery; comes out again, and watches the* DOCTOR *go. The* DOCTOR *pulls the white muffler closer around his neck, settles his hat more firmly on his head, giving a few thick coughs as he does so, and goes out of the waiting-room. Giving a richer belch as he goes out by the door.*) Jasus, I'm in a terrible state!

ALLELUIA *shuts the Surgery door and locks it, putting the key in his pocket. He goes to the Dispensary door and locks that too. He sees the three bottles on the floor that* GREEN MUFFLER *left behind him. He takes them up and shoves them under the bench, singing the chorus of 'The Rose of Tralee' as he does these things. The organ is heard softly playing its old tune; it comes faintly into the room, as if to counterpoint the song sung by* ALLELUIA.

ALLELUIA (*singing, and breaking off at times, resuming again when his breathing finds it convenient*):

She was lovelee an' fayer as ay ... rose ... bud in summer.
But it was not ... her beaut ... tee aylone than won ... me;
Ah, no, 'twas they trewth in her ... eyes fondly beam ... in',
That mayed me love Mary, they rose of
   *He is now at the entrance door; he gives a last look round, then goes out, closing the door behind him. Outside the door*
Traa ... leee!

AS THE CURTAIN FALLS

# It Should Happen to a Dog

*Wolf Mankowitz (1924-    )*

## Characters

Jonah
A Man
A Sailor
The King
An Angel

## EDITOR'S NOTE

This little play is notable for the imaginative simplicity of its staging and its use of a regional accent and habits of speech, so typical of much of the new British drama. Like Arnold Wesker, Harold Pinter and Bernard Kops, Wolf Mankowitz grew up in the Jewish East End of London, and he has drawn on its characters and its dialect in such plays as *The Bespoke Overcoat* and the film *A Kid for Two Farthings*. He has written the following note on this play:

'*It Should Happen to a Dog* is a serio-comic strip, which, those who know the story of Jonah will see, is faithful to the original. If the characters speak as people we know personally, it is because there is no other way for us to know characters. If Jonah is somewhat familiar in his manner of address to the Almighty—it is because one may assume that a greater intimacy exists between Prophets and their source of instruction than does for the rest of us.

'In the staging of *It Should Happen to a Dog,* a coat-stand is required from which the rope of the ship is hung, and upon which any practical props may also hang. The coat-stand becomes the tree in the last scene, and should be placed behind Jonah's back in full view of the audience by the Angel or by a property man who may be written-in at the director's discretion. A thunder-sheet will be found useful. The characters should be dressed in an ana-chronistic selection of garments suggestive of our own time and of biblical times, and the piece should be played at a fast tempo.

'As to the message of the story—"Why should I not spare Nineveh?"—this is, one hopes, how God feels about Man —unlike Man who is less tolerant of himself.'

# IT SHOULD HAPPEN TO A DOG

## SCENE I

JONAH (*talking to Someone in the sky*): Please, please, what do you want from my life? (*To audience*) He won't leave me alone. All these years I've been running—a traveller—Jonah, the traveller, representing Top Hat; Braces For The Trousers; Fair Lady Fancy Buttons; Hold Tight grips—only good brands in the suitcase. Ask them in Tarshish, ask them in Aleppo, in Carthage even; they all know Jonah ben Amittai, regular call once a month for more than thirty years. I don't complain, only I'm tired of running, that's all. Now at last I'm tired. I get this good pitch here—at last—so I shouldn't have to run with a suitcase any more. And still he nags me. (*To Someone above*) All right. I heard. I'm going. (*To himself*) What happens to me shouldn't happen to a dog.

*A* MAN *stands in his way.*

MAN: It's a nice pitch you got here.

JONAH: It's nice.

MAN: So what are you looking so down in the mouth for?

JONAH: What's the use of talking? It has to happen to me.

MAN: What happens?

JONAH: This dream.

MAN: Dream?

JONAH: I tell you, this is a most terrible dream. The voice comes like the voice of a bird. In the middle hours of the night it comes chirping, chirping, 'The end of the world is at hand. The end of the world is at hand'.

MAN: Could be right. It wouldn't be the first time.

64

JONAH: So all right then, let it be the end of the world. Is it my business? Am I to blame?

MAN: And this is *all* the voice says?

JONAH (*lying*): Certainly that's all. Isn't it enough? What else should it say?

MAN: Nothing. Only if that is all the voice says you got nothing to worry about. Look—if it *is* the end of the world, what can you do? On the other hand—if it isn't —you got nothing to worry about. I'll take a quarter ounce Archangel Gabriel tobacco.

JONAH (*handing him a small packet of tobacco*): That's a good brand. I opened up the Tarshish territory for Archangel Gabriel.

MAN: I never smoke nothing else. (*Starts to go.*)

JONAH: Ay, ay.

MAN: Oh. (*Giving coin*) Chirp, chirp? (*Laughing*) Chirp, chirp, heh, heh ... (*as he goes out*).

JONAH: I hate birds. You know what it says? 'Arise, Jonah, arise. Go to Nineveh, that great city, and cry against it.' I ask you. Why pick on me? Why sort me out? Chirp, chirp. It's in my head the whole time. Once I could sleep fifteen hours—like a short course of death. No more. I hate birds. (*To God*) All right, I'm going—to the docks—for a ship.

*He walks into the next area and set-up.*

SCENE II

*A* SAILOR *is untying a rope from a capstan as* JONAH *enters.*

JONAH (*to God*): Certainly I'm on my way. By ship. You expect me to fly? If you are so clever and in such a hurry, make me sprout a couple of wings so I'll take off. It's quicker by air. But so far is only invented the ship. (*To the* SAILOR) Which way you going, shipmate?

SAILOR: Tarshish.

JONAH: You don't say. I got a lot of friends there. It's a beautiful place. In Tarshish they got more people over a hundred years old than anywhere else.

SAILOR: Who wants to live so long?

JONAH: In some circumstances, chirp, chirp, who gets a chance to live so long? Tarshish, eh? (*Aside*) It seems silly, if I'm going all this way to Nineveh (where I am certainly eventually going) why don't I break my journey and look up a few old friends in Tarshish. Why not? It's a crime? (*To the* SAILOR) You can take passengers?

SAILOR: First class or tourist?

JONAH: In the old days when I was travelling for myself, nothing but first class for J. B. Amittai. But in these circumstances, one tourist.

SAILOR: Single or return?

JONAH: What's the matter with you? Return, of course. I got a wonderful little business waiting for me when I come back.

SAILOR (*shouts*): One more tourist coming up. Tarshish return.

JONAH (*aside, as he begins to board ship*): I'll spend a couple of days there to build my strength up and then I'll give such a shout against Nineveh. After all, it's a tough territory, and what difference can a couple of days make? Thank you. (*Sits*) Oh, it's a beautiful day for sailing. Any more for the Skylark?

*Black Out*

### SCENE III

JONAH *asleep on some bales of goods. The* SAILOR *wakes him.*

JONAH: Chirp, chirp. The end of the world is at hand. (*He wakes up.*)

SAILOR: If it isn't troubling you.

JONAH: The weather's come over black all of a sudden.

SAILOR: In all my years I never knew a storm this time of the year.

JONAH: Are we far from Tarshish?

SAILOR: Are you barmy? We been stuck out here for the past five hours, and all the wind does is try to blow us back. In all my years I never see anything like it.

JONAH: Very interesting phenomena. Like St. Ermin's fire; caused by electricity in the atmosphere, you understand? And take the sea serpent, for example.

SAILOR: I will.

JONAH: The sea serpent is really a very big eel. Science proves it.

SAILOR: I don't take any chances. After I tried every trick I know, I pray. (*He prays for a few moments. Then he looks at* JONAH.) You too, guv'ner.

JONAH: I already said my prayers today. To duplicate is just silly. When it comes to the evening I'll say my evening prayers.

SAILOR: Don't take no chances. Pray now.

JONAH: It should happen to a dog what happens to me. Listen, God. Stop messing me about. Didn't I give you my word of honour I will go to Nineveh? Ask anybody anywhere in these territories. Jonah's word is his bond.

*A gale begins to blew.*

Do me a favour just this once. I will catch the first boat from Tarshish to Nineveh. The very first boat.

*The gale blows stronger.*

SAILOR: Did you make a sacrifice yet? We got all the passengers making sacrifices to all the different gods. That way we must hit the right god sooner or later and he'll stop the storm. Guv'ner, did you make a sacrifice yet?

JONAH: Here. I sacrifice this beautiful meat pie. I only ate a small portion of it.

SAILOR: Right. Throw it overboard with an appropriate prayer.

JONAH: Here, God. And remember I'm catching the first boat from Tarshish. All right?

*He throws the pie overboard. The pie is thrown straight back, and JONAH catches it. The SAILOR looks at him significantly, then calls out.*

SAILOR: Aye, aye. This is it, folks.

JONAH: It's a perfectly natural phenomena.

SAILOR: This man is the trouble-maker.

JONAH: It's got a perfectly natural explanation.

SAILOR: His sacrifice was definitely refused. He's the one. Overboard with him—overboard. (*He advances on* JONAH)

JONAH: You can't do this to me. I am on very important business. I can drown in there. What happens to me should happen to a dog.

*He backs away from the influence of the SAILOR till he falls overboard and the gale stops and the sun comes out.*

SAILOR: I never did like the look of that fella. To me, he always looked a trouble-maker. Uh? What? (*He follows the progress of* JONAH *in the water.*) You could live a thousand years, you wouldn't see a man swallowed by a whale. But who would believe such a story?

*Black Out*

SCENE IV

JONAH (*gropes in the dark, then strikes a match*): Faugh—
it smells like Billingsgate in here. All right. Now what
am I supposed to do. Now I can't go to Nineveh. All I
wanted to do was to go to Nineveh and cry against it,
and look at me. Maybe I'm dead. I must be dead. Who
would have thought that being dead was a black-out in
a fish shop? Maybe *this is* the end of the world. But if
it isn't, if, for example, don't laugh, I happen to have
been swallowed by a whale, tee-hee, I categorically put
it on record that if I could go to Nineveh at this moment
I would definitely and unconditionally go to Nineveh at
this moment.

*A crash of thunder; lightning.* JONAH *executes a double
somersault into the light. Looks around, amazed.*

Honestly, God, sometimes I can't make you out. You've
got such a mysterious way of carrying on. (*He stretches
himself*) So where's Tarshish? Tarshish. (*Disgusted*) If
I'm not dead and if I'm not mistaken and if my memory
serves me right that great city in the distance is—
*Nineveh.* It should happen to a dog. (*Exit, towards
Nineveh.*)

SCENE V

KING (*enters, sits, sorts papers, looks up*): Jonah B. Amittai.
JONAH: Yes, Your Majesty.
KING: You are up on a charge of vagrancy.
JONAH: Uh?
KING: Vagrancy.
JONAH: Oh.
KING: Also it seems you have been talking a lot of sedi-
tious nonsense about the end of the world is at hand.

Also—what's this? Also you keep saying 'chirp, chirp'. This official work is beginning to get me down. All night long I get the most terrible dreams. Mmm—what have you got to say for yourself?

JONAH: Just a minute. (*He mounts the throne and sings*) The Lord saith: Cry out against Nineveh, that great city, for their wickedness is come up before me. Stop. Yet forty days and Nineveh shall be overthrown. Stop. The end of the world is at hand. Stop. Repent lest ye perish. End of message. And that, Your Majesty, in short, is what I am instructed to tell you. (*Sits*) Personally it makes no difference to me. I should be just as pleased for Nineveh not to be destroyed. For my part it can go on being as wicked as you like, though, if you was to ask my opinion, as a business man of some experience, I'll tell you straight out that honesty is always the best policy. A satisfied client is better than Government consuls. Especially as, I am instructed to tell you, the Government is not going to last too long, anyway.

KING: What's the source of your information?

JONAH: A little bird tells me every night.

KING (*alarmed*): A bird?

JONAH: A little bird. Chirp, chirp. It makes just like that.

KING: What colour the feathers?

JONAH: The feathers! One wing is blue, the other wing white, the breast red, the tail purple, but the funny thing is, this bird has one brown eye and—

KING: —and the other a blue!

JONAH: You are familiar with it?

KING: I have been getting the same dream.

JONAH: Oh. So *your* little bird tells *me* one hundred times nightly to come to Nineveh and inform *you* that in forty days from now *you* are completely in liquidation. And that's what *I'm* telling *you*? It's a madhouse here!

KING (*stands up and tears his robe*): Let neither man nor beast, herd nor flock, taste anything. Let them not eat food nor drink water; but let man and beast be covered with sack-cloth and cry mightily unto God. Yea, let them turn every one from his evil way, and from the violence that is in their hands. Let them turn from the violence that is in their hands for the sake of the smallest bird, for the bird also is God. (*To* JONAH) Who can tell if God will turn and repent, and turn away from his fierce anger, that we perish not?

JONAH: Who can tell? But if you ask my opinion, I don't think so. Otherwise he doesn't go to all this trouble. No, king, this is the end. Still, you can always try. There's no charge for trying. (*Exeunt*)

*Blackout*

SCENE VI

JONAH *is sitting on a rock in the scorching sun. In the background a celebratory fair-ground noise, like a Bank Holiday Monday.*

JONAH: It should happen to a dog, what happens to me. Here after all this the King himself takes my personal word that in forty days it is the end of the world; and what happens? The forty-first day is proclaimed a national holiday. Government stock rises, and I am the biggest fool in the Middle East. I am a laughing stock, that's all, a laughing stock. I don't move. I'm going to sit here until I get sun-stroke. You can do what you like with Nineveh, Miniver, Shminever. I'm finished. 'Yet forty days and Nineveh shall be overthrown.'

*Laughter off and voices singing: 'Jonah, Jonah—he pulled a boner.'*

71

Listen to 'em. Laugh your heads off! Three-four hours I won't hear you any more. And I won't hear that damned bird either no more. I hate birds.

*A shadow is thrown over* JONAH.

What's this? By my life. A tree!

*A palm tree has sprung up from nowhere. He reaches down a coconut.*

What do you know? Coconuts as well with a patent zipper. You just pull it open and drink the milk. Ice cold. Delicous. And what's this. The *Tarshish Gazette*. Well, this is certainly a novelty. (*Reads*) Aha. I see that Mrs. Zinkin has been presented with her third daughter. That's bad. Young Fyvel is opening a café espresso bar on the High Street. That's a good position. He should do well. It's just like a summer holiday here now, and believe me, I earned a vacation. This is certainly a wonderful place you made here, Lord. I got to hand it to you. For land development you're the tops.

*Standing beside him is an angel.* JONAH *sees him and looks away, back to his paper.*

ANGEL: A beautiful day.

JONAH: Yes, it's certainly marvellous weather we're having.

ANGEL: That's a remarkable palm tree. (*He reaches out for a coconut.*) This I never saw before.

JONAH: It's got a zipper.

ANGEL: What will he think of next, eh? (*He offers the coconut to the irritable* JONAH.)

JONAH (*throwing down the newspaper*): All right. Cut out the performance. You are an angel, right?

ANGEL: I must give you credit, Jonah. You're certainly quick off the mark.

JONAH: But an angel?

72

ANGEL: Archangel.

JONAH: Oh—so now what do I have to do? Go back to Nineveh? Tell the King the Lord has changed his mind again? He is going to give him ten more days and then bring the world to an end? He made a laughing stock of me.

ANGEL: What can you do?

JONAH: Admitted. But at the same time this is a terrible way to treat someone who goes through all the trouble I go through. For what—only He knows. And He won't tell. (*Turns, bangs into tree*) Feh! Fancy trees yet!

ANGEL (*wheedling*): That's certainly a *wonderful* tree. Help yourself.

JONAH: Perhaps just another coconut. These coconuts are delicious.

*As he turns the tree withers, collapsing into dust; that is, the coatstand is removed.*

What a terrible thing to happen. Such a wonderful tree. With such trees mankind could live in plenty for ever. A quick death from some palm tree disease, I suppose?

ANGEL: It's a small worm crawls through the arterial system of the tree, cuts off the life from the heart. And boom.

JONAH: A quick death to that worm.

ANGEL: Ah. You notice something. How annoyed you are with this worm which after all only killed a tree, which after all didn't cause you an hour's work. After all, you don't hear God complain; He made the tree to come up in a night. He can make it go down the night after.

JONAH: It cranks me such a beautiful tree should die like that, apart from now I am in the sun again and can catch a sun stroke any minute. Pity about the tree. Hey-

73

hey. This is some kind of parable, ain't it? You are trying to teach me something, isn't it?

ANGEL: That's my boy. By this little experiment He is saying, if you feel sorry for the tree, which after all didn't cost you anything, why shouldn't He feel sorry for Nineveh, that great city, in which there are one hundred and twenty thousand human beings on whom after all He has taken a great deal of trouble even if they still don't know what time it is, or their left hand from their right hand. Also much cattle.

JONAH: You got a point there, there was never any harm in those cattle. But if you don't mind a question ...

ANGEL: Any help I can give you.

JONAH: If God knew right from the start exactly what He is going to do about everything—right?

ANGEL: That's right.

JONAH: Then He knows He isn't going to destroy Nineveh. Right?

ANGEL: Right!

JONAH: Then what does He want of my life? What's the point of all this expensive business with whales and palm trees and so on?

ANGEL: You mankind, you can't see no further than your nose.

JONAH: So what's the answer?

ANGEL: You see—(*long pause*)—frankly, I don't know.

JONAH: It should happen to a dog.

ANGEL: Me too. After all, it's no joke following you or any other prophet I happen to get assigned to around the whole time. You think it's such a wonderful thing to be an angel and do a few conjuring tricks? It *should* happen to a dog.

JONAH: On the other hand, come to think of it, whose dogs are we?

74

ANGEL: We are the dogs of God.

JONAH: So ...

ANGEL: Well?

JONAH: Whatever happens to a dog ...

ANGEL: ... must happen to us, eh? (*He chuckles with admiration.*)

JONAH: Can you give me a lift back home?

ANGEL: It's a pleasure.

JONAH *jumps on* ANGEL'S *back.*

JONAH: On the way we could call in at Tarshish. I got a lot of friends there.

ANGEL: That's a good idea. So have I. (*As they go out*) Did you hear that young Fyvel opened a café espresso bar on the High Street?

JONAH: I read it in the paper. He's a clever boy.

**CURTAIN**

# The New Tenant

*Eugène Ionesco (1912-    )*

translated by

*Donald Watson*

## Characters

The  Gentleman
The  Caretaker
The  1st Furniture Remover
The  2nd Furniture Remover

# EDITOR'S NOTE

Before discussing exactly what this play means, let us examine its effect in the theatre. It proceeds like some pedantic ritual, with a quiet, unhurried gentleman directing operations. During the course of them, our eyes and our ears register that two extraordinary things are happening. What we see is an empty stage filling slowly but inexorably with furniture, filling up like a tank with water, till there is not an inch left to move in. Simultaneously we *hear* an indescribable din (hammering and shouting off-stage, and a Caretaker talking non-stop on stage) which all sinks gradually away to stillness and silence—the silence of the grave. The gentleman can no longer be seen for the furniture. He has, quite deliberately, had himself buried.

It is an eerie thing to watch, and even when reading it you must imagine yourself watching it. For this reason we have printed the principal stage-directions in such a way that they can be readily distinguished from minor directions and from the dialogue itself. In a reading, these directions should be spoken aloud by a fifth actor as an essential part of the action. But when you see it all happening, it becomes obvious that this play is not, like ordinary plays, telling a story, but is a *symbol* of something, something much easier felt than put into words. The gentleman, I suggested, had 'had himself buried'. Not literally, of course, but symbolically—buried away from the world, shut off from reality and life (vulgar, noisy life as represented by the Caretaker). Perhaps he symbolizes that feel-

78

ing all of us have sometimes, of wanting to run away and hide from everything and everybody. At the same time he has this obsession with furniture. He must have all his personal bric-à-brac around him, the sort of senseless lumber that people accumulate during their lives and hoard in attics and cupboards and cellars and cannot bear to throw away. The world, Ionesco seems to say, is full of men like this one, who attach more value to things than to people; who (because they are frightened of life? because they are lonely?) bury themselves in cluttered rooms or—to put it in a more symbolic way— shut themselves up in their own thoughts, the furniture of their minds.

Symbols, like poetry, cannot be wholly explained. If they could, there would be no need to use them. Neither can this play, but as in a poem we can sense the hidden truth in it. This sort of drama, puzzling but somehow significant, has made Ionesco one of the most talked-about and argued-about playwrights in the world today. He is Rumanian by birth, but lives in Paris and writes in French. He is the main exponent of what is called the 'Theatre of the Absurd', for his symbolic parables use illogical means to depict human behaviour as itself illogical. Very sane men often seem to regard the world as more than a little mad—a place, for example, where heavy furniture can appear light and light furniture heavy; where, if you once get obsessed with anything so unreasonable as shutting yourself up in a room full of lumber, the whole process could snowball till furniture comes sliding in of its own accord or piles up on the staircase, in the yard, in the street, in the Underground. This last little vision is the play's most frightening moment. It has the absurdity of nightmare.

The play should be acted with a carefully controlled

pace, as if it were gradually slowing down; starting loud and fast, with the Caretaker gabbling on and on, and getting steadily quieter and more deliberate, till the curtain comes down as a natural full stop. It is easiest to attempt on a very small stage, then less bric-à-brac is needed to fill it.

# THE NEW TENANT

[SCENE: A bare room, without any furniture. In the centre of the back wall, an open window. Double doors on the right and on the left. Light coloured walls. Like the set and the furniture that will be brought on the stage later, the style of acting must be completely realistic. As the CURTAIN RISES, a considerable din is heard off-stage: the sounds of VOICES and HAMMERS, snatches of SONG, CHILDREN SHOUTING, the NOISE OF FEET going up and coming down stairs, a BARREL ORGAN, and so on. For a moment, as the noise goes on, the stage is empty; then THE CARETAKER comes in from the right, crashing the door open and singing in a loud voice; she is holding a bunch of keys.]

CARETAKER (*as she enters, singing*): La, la, la, tralalala, tralali, tralalalala-a-a! (*rattling the keys*) La, la, la, la, (*Interrupts her singing to go and lean out of the open window*) Bill! Oh, Bill! Bill! Hullo there, George! Go and tell Bill 'e's got to see Mr. Clarence! ... George ... (*no reply*) George ... (*no reply*) Well! If 'e ain't missing too! (*She tries to lean still further out of the window, singing at the top of her voice*) La, la, la, la, la, la, la!

[While the row continues and the CARETAKER is still craning out of the

window, the GENTLEMAN comes silently
in from the left: he is middle-aged,
with a little black moustache,
dressed in dark clothes; he is wearing
a bowler hat, black jacket and striped
trousers, his shoes are of patent
leather, he is carrying gloves, and
an overcoat over one arm, and he
has a little attaché case of black
leather. He closes the door quietly
behind him and walks silently up to
the CARETAKER, who does not notice
him. He stops beside her and waits
for an instant without moving. The
CARETAKER suddenly stops singing as
she becomes aware of the stranger's
presence: but she does not look round
till the GENTLEMAN speaks.

GENTLEMAN: Excuse me, are you the caretaker?

CARETAKER (*putting her hand to her heart, she cries out*):
Oh! oh! oh! (*Then she hiccups.*) I beg pardon, sir. I've
got the hiccups.

[The GENTLEMAN does not stir.]

'Ave you only just come in?

GENTLEMAN: Just this moment.

CARETAKER: I was tryin' to see if Bill—or George perhaps
—or someone else anyway, was in the yard ... It's about
going to see Mr. Clarence. Well! ... so you've arrived
then?

GENTLEMAN: As you can see.

CARETAKER: I wasn't expectin' you, not for today I wasn't
... I thought you was meant to come tomorrow ...
Pleased to see you, anyway. Did you 'ave a good

journey? Not too tired, I 'ope? Give me quite a turn, you did! I suppose you got finished sooner than you expected! That must be it. It's just because it took me by surprise, like. (*She hiccups.*) It's the hiccups. Shock, you know. It's only what you might expect. Good thing the last lot—the people what was 'ere before you, you know—moved everything out in time. I'm not sure as 'ow I know what he used to do, mind. They said they'd send me some postcards. Worked for the government. Not a bit nervy, 'e wasn't. I suppose you wouldn't be? Would you? Don't know what department 'e worked for. I've forgot. 'E told me once. Me and them government departments! And my first 'usband was an office-boy. They was good folks. Used to tell me everything, they did. I get used to folks' little secrets, I do. Mum's the word for me! 'Er—the old lady, I mean—she didn't used to work. Never lifted a finger in 'er life. I used to look after the place for 'em, she used to 'ave someone in to run errands for 'er and when she didn't used to come, it was me again! (*She hiccups.*) What a fright you gave me! I wasn't expectin' you till tomorrow. Or the day after. Used to have a little dog, they did, they 'ated cats, but then cats isn't allowed in this establishment. 'Course it's all the same to me, it's the landlord what says so! Regular sort of folk they were—no children, of course—off they'd go to the country every Sunday to some cousins of theirs, 'olidays in Devonshire, that's where the old gentleman come from, that's where they've gone to live now, but they didn't used to like the cider they 'ave there—said it used to go to their heads, liked a drop of port now and again, just a drop, of course—*old* they were, even when they were young—well, there it is, we 'aven't all got the same ideas, 'ave we? Take me, for instance. I'm not like that. Still, they was nice folks. And what about you? In business, are you? Clerk? Got your own money, perhaps? Pension? Oh, but not yet, you're too young for that, though you never know, some of them give up early when they've *got* a little money, 'course everybody can't, good luck to them that can, that's what I say. Got any family?

GENTLEMAN (*laying his case and overcoat on the floor*): No, I'm afraid not.

CARETAKER: That's right, put your case down. Nice bit of leather—mustn't 'ave an Irishman's rest! You can put it where you like. Well I'm blowed! 'Iccups 'ave gone! Got over me fright! Why don't you take your 'at off and make yourself comfortable?

> [The GENTLEMAN adjusts his hat more
> firmly on his head.]

Oh, I shouldn't bother to take your 'at off, sir. Of course, you're at 'ome now, aren't you? Last week it wasn't your 'ome yet—there's always change—it was *their* 'ome —well, can't be helped—you 'ave to get old—it's all a question of age—now this is *your* 'ome, I'm not the one to say it ain't—very nice 'ere it is, a good 'ouse—must be twenty years now—my, that's a good long stretch ...

> [Without saying a word, the GENTLE-
> MAN takes a few paces in the empty
> room and looks around carefully, at
> the walls, the doors, the ceiling; now
> he has his hands behind his back.]

Ooh! They left everything proper, sir! Clean folks they was, really nice people. Mm? Well, of course they 'ad their faults like you and me—bit proud they was and not what you might call talkative, not talkative by a long chalk—never said anything much about anything to me, they didn't—only silly things—'im—the old 'un,

I mean—well, 'e was what you might call all right—but 'er, not 'er—threw 'er cat out of the window, she did— 'it the landlord on the 'ead—what a thud!—still, didn't 'urt my flowers. And as for 'im, 'e didn't 'arf used to beat 'er, if you can believe it, sir, in these days—oh, that was their business—didn't go poking my nose in— when I come up once, 'e was going for 'er with 'is fists, something awful—screaming she was, 'you brute! You 'orrible beast!' (*She bursts out laughing*).

> [But the GENTLEMAN is having a closer
> look at the state of the walls, still
> without uttering a word; he inspects
> the doors and the locks, moves his
> hand over them, shakes his head,
> while the CARETAKER watches every
> movement as she goes on talking;
> the din outside continues.]

Oh, I 'ad to laugh, sir—but there, they're away now, mustn't tell tales—just as though they was dead, not *just* the same p'raps, specially as it's all the same really —very nice they was, can't say I 'ad anything to grumble about, except for New Year's Day ... Oh, don't you go worrying yourself about the 'ouse, sir, *that's* sound enough—this 'ouse wasn't born yesterday, don't make 'em like that nowadays ... You'll be all right 'ere, that you will ... the neighbours are good folk, it's all 'armony 'ere, always nice and quiet—I've never once 'ad to call the police in, 'cept for the third floor front —Hinspector 'e is, shouts out all the time, wants to arrest everybody, 'e does ...

GENTLEMAN (*pointing*): I beg your pardon, the window! (*In an even expressionless tone of voice.*)

CARETAKER: Oh, but of course, sir—I'm only too willing to

do for you. I don't ask very much, sir. Get on fine, you
an' me will, you won't 'ave any insurance stamps to
worry you ...

GENTLEMAN (*same gesture, same calm*): The window,
please!

CARETAKER: Oh yes, sir, I am sorry—I *was* forgettin'.

> [As she closes the window, there is a
> little less noise to be heard.]

... You know 'ow it is, sir, one word leads to the next
and don't time fly?

> [The GENTLEMAN continues his inspec-
> tion.]

I've closed the window for you, just as you wanted—
closes nice and easy.

> [The GENTLMAN inspects the window
> fasteners and the window itself.]

Of course it looks out on the yard, but it's nice and
bright as you can see, that's because it's on the sixth
floor ...

GENTLEMAN: There was nothing available on the ground
floor.

CARETAKER: Oh! Don't think I don't know what you mean
—it's no joke, the sixth floor, not when there's no lift ...

GENTLEMAN (*rather to himself*): That's not the point. I'm
not at all tired.

CARETAKER: Oh, I see. Then why, sir? ... I suppose you
don't like the sun? 'Course, it's true it can 'urt your eyes!
When you get to a certain age, you can get on quite
well without it, burns your skin right off, it does ...

GENTLEMAN: Not at all.

CARETAKER: Well, not *right* off, of course. You 'aven't anything to sleep on tonight, 'ave you? I can lend you a
bed!

[For some minutes the GENTLEMAN, still engrossed in his examination of the room, has been deciding where to put the furniture that will be arriving, pointing out to himself the various position. He takes a tape-measure out of his pocket and starts measuring.]

I'll 'elp you to arrange the furniture, don't you worry about that, I'll give you some ideas—plenty of them about—won't be the first time, neither—since I'm going to look after you—you won't see it come today, your furniture, at any rate, they won't be bringing it as quick as that, just you see, I know all their little tricks, them tradespeople's all the same ...

GENTLEMAN: Yes indeed.

CARETAKER: *You* think they're going to bring all your things today, do you? No 'arm in *thinking*—suits me all right, I've got no bed to lend you, but mind it'd surprise *me*, 'cause I *know* 'em. My, but I've seen 'em before, this lot's not the first, they won't come, you mark my words, it's Saturday—no, it ain't, it's a Wednesday— I've got a bed for you ... since I'm going to do for you ...

[She goes to open the window.]

GENTLEMAN: If you don't mind!

CARETAKER: What's the matter? I've got to call George to tell 'im to tell Bill to go and see Mr. Clarence ...

GENTLEMAN: Leave the window alone, please.

CARETAKER: It's all on account of Mr. Clarence, what wants to know if Mr. Eustace, who's a friend of Bill and George's too, since they're what you might call relations, not exactly, but in a kind of way ...

87

GENTLEMAN: Please leave the window alone.

CARETAKER: All right, all right, I 'eard you, you don't want me to—wouldn't 'ave done no 'arm—you're in your rights of course, it's your window, not mine. I don't want no window—I get you, it's you gives the orders, it's just as *you* like, I won't touch it, you're the boss in your own place—don't pay much for it either— still, no business of mine—the window, that's yours, too, you can buy anything when you've got a spot of money, that's life for you—I don't say nothing. I keeps to myself, it's your affair—'ave to go down six flights of stairs now to look for Bill, poor old woman like me—Ah, well! Can't 'elp men 'aving their little ways, don't think about nothing they don't—but I'll do just what you like, you know, it's all right with me, that don't worry me, suits me fine that does, I'm going to look after you, be as though I was your servant, like, won't it, sir?

GENTLEMAN: No, I'm afraid it won't.

CARETAKER: Beg pardon, sir?

GENTLEMAN: I shan't be needing your services, I'm afraid.

CARETAKER: Well, I like that! After all the time you've been asking me to do for you! Bit of bad luck I didn't 'ave no witness, took you at your word, I did, got proper took in ... Too kind 'earted, that's me ...

GENTLEMAN: I beg your pardon. Please don't get upset about it.

CARETAKER: Well, that's all right then.

[There is a knock at the door on the left.]

GENTLEMAN: The furniture!

CARETAKER: I'll open the door. Don't you disturb yourself. I'm the one to open the door. Must wait on you, you know. I'm your servant.

[She goes to open the door, but the GENTLEMAN steps in front of her and stops her.]

GENTLEMAN (*still very calmly*): Please don't do anything like that!

[He walks to the door and opens it while the CARETAKER, hands on hips exclaims:]

CARETAKER: Well, that's a bit of all right! They make up to you, promise you the 'ole world, and then they go back on their word!

[The GENTLEMAN opens the door and the FIRST FURNITURE MOVER comes in.]

1st MOVER: 'Day to you!
GENTLEMAN: Is the furniture here?
1st MOVER: Can we bring it up?
GENTLEMAN: Yes, if you like.
1st MOVER: Very well, sir.

[He goes out.]

CARETAKER: You won't never be able to arrange all that furniture by yourself, sir.
GENTLEMAN: That will be all right. I shall have the removal men to help me.
CARETAKER: Well, you 'ardly want *strangers* to do it, do you? I don't even know that one, I've never seen 'im before, it's not safe! You ought to 'ave asked my 'ubby. Ought never to have let 'im come in, don't do to trust no-one—you never know, you know, that's just 'ow things 'appen—foolish I call it when there's my old man, my second you know, don't know what 'appened to the first—he's down below, got nothing to do, 'asn't

89

got a job—'e's 'efty enough you know, would 'elp 'im to earn a bit, why give your money away to other people, it don't do no good, 'e could bring it up all right, 'e's tubercular you know, still, got to earn 'is bit, 'asn't 'e? Them strikers is right, so was my first 'ubby, 'e'd 'ad enough of it, so off 'e went and then everyone's surprised!—Oh well, I'm not a bad sort really, you know, I'll look after you, wouldn't mind looking after you at all ...

GENTLEMAN: I'm afraid I really shan't be needing your services. I'm extremely sorry. I shall be looking after myself, you see.

CARETAKER (*losing her temper and shouting*): 'E says 'e's sorry, does 'e! Thinks 'e can do what he likes, does 'e! —Oooh! I don't like these sort of goings on, you can't make no fool out of me! I wish the old couple 'adn't gone, they weren't like that at all. As kind and obliging as you could wish for! They're all alike, one's as bad as another! Make you waste all your time, as though I 'adn't got nothing else to do! Tells me to come up, 'e does, and then ...

> [The noise increases off-stage, especially the sound of hammers. The GENTLEMAN pulls a wry face. The CARETAKER screams out into the wings.]

Don't make so much noise! I can't 'ear myself speak. (*To the* GENTLEMAN) It's all right, I'm not going to open your window, I don't want to break nobody's windowpanes—I'm respectable, I am, no-one never 'ad anything to say about that—So I've been wasting my time, 'ave I?—and all that washing to do, better for me if I 'adn't listened to you!

[The door opens noisily and lets the
1ST FURNITURE MOVER appear, carrying
two very small stools, while the CARE-
TAKER's tirade goes on.]

1ST MOVER: Here's the first lot, anyway!

CARETAKER (to 1ST MOVER, who takes no notice): Don't you
believe a word 'e says, my lad ...

1ST MOVER (to GENTLEMAN): Where shall I put them?

CARETAKER: ... A pack of lies, you needn't think 'e'll pay
you for it, think they can buy everything with money!

GENTLEMAN (calmly): Would you mind putting one of
them there? And one there!

[He points either side of the left-hand
door.]

CARETAKER (as before): 'E'll make you sweat, 'e will.

1ST MOVER: Very good, sir.

[He sets them down as directed.]

CARETAKER: ... Work yourself to death, that's all life is
for the likes of us ...

[The FURNITURE MOVER goes out. The
CARETAKER turns towards the GENTLE-
MAN.]

I don't know who you *are*, but I know who *I* am. I
know your sort ... Mrs. Fairchild, that's me.

GENTLEMAN (still calm, taking money from pocket): Please
take this for your trouble!

CARETAKER: Well, I never! Who do you take me for? ...
I'm no pauper, wasn't my fault if I couldn't 'ave any
kids, that's on account of my old man, they'd be grown
up now, they would—I don't want your money! (takes
it and puts it in her apron pocket) Very good of you,
I'm sure, sir! ... No! It's no good, you can make as

much fuss as you like, you won't catch me looking after you, not the likes of you, you won't, your sort's not for me—'e don't need no-one, 'e don't, wants to do it all for 'isself, 'e does— fine thing that is, too, at your time o' life ...

> [She rambles on while the GENTLEMAN walks calmly to the door, changes round the two stools and moves back to judge the effect.]

... a bad lot, that's what 'e is, a bad lot in the 'ouse, don't need nobody 'e don't, not even a blessed dog to keep 'im company—that's the sort that prowls round the streets at night—what a time to live in! Never wanted nobody like that, I didn't, fine state of affairs, we only 'ave respectable folks in our 'ouse— (*still louder*) —that's the sort that frightens folks on purpose when they're looking out of the window, might have broken my neck and don't need nothing 'e don't. Only wanted to pass the time o' day, don't do no one no harm, don't get much fun I don't, 'cept the pictures now and again and that's about all, don't even know what they want, they don't ... don't know much about life, that sort don't, don't do nothing but kick up a fuss ...

GENTLEMAN (*inspecting the stools with a satisfied look, but he is too phlegmatic to show much emotion*): Yes, they're better that way!

> [The 1st FURNITURE MOVER comes in through the same door, noisily, with a vase in his hand.]

CARETAKER: Don't 'alf 'ave a fine opinion of themselves either, they do—nothing but a lot of thieves, louts and good-for-nothings ...

GENTLEMAN (*to 1st* MOVER): Here, you may put it here.

> [He points to the left-hand corner of the stage, at the back.]

1st MOVER: There? Very good, sir!

CARETAKER: Makes all sorts of shameful suggestions to you, they does—for money ...

GENTLEMAN: No! In the corner, right in the corner, there ...

CARETAKER: That sort of lark don't cut no ice with me, not with me, it don't!

1st MOVER: Here?

GENTLEMAN: Yes, there, it's fine like that ...

CARETAKER: Oh, no! Money don't buy everything, money don't pervert everyone ... *I* won't 'ave it any'ow!

1st MOVER (*to the* GENTLEMAN): But where are you going to put the rest?

GENTLEMAN: Oh, please don't trouble about that, I've thought it all out, you'll see, there'll be room ...

> [The FURNITURE MOVER goes out.]

CARETAKER: Not that it's not what I weren't expecting, your sort don't catch me napping, I know 'em, I do, all of them fine gentlemen prowling round the streets, I've got my eyes open, I 'ave, you don't catch me 'aving any, run after anything in a skirt they will, but they don't 'ave me on! I know what you're up to, I know your little game. Fine cheek you 'ave, come making nasty suggestions to a mother, with five kids too—I'm not so daft as you think I am, I've got my 'ead screwed on all right, good thing for me I 'ave. Listen 'ere, sir, there's a police hinspector lives right in this very 'ouse, I'll charge you, I will, I'll 'ave you arrested, and then there's my old man too to look after my hinterests ... Oh, no! Don't need nobody, 'e don't, eh? We'll see about that!

[The GENTLEMAN does not raise his
voice and keeps his dignity perfectly,
but he gives a surprising impression
of authority as he turns towards the
CARETAKER.]

GENTLEMAN: Please don't upset yourself! Take my advice
and accept my apologies; otherwise you will only make
yourself ill!

CARETAKER (*somewhat intimidated*): How dare you talk
to me like that! To me! Mother of five children! You
won't 'ave me on like that, you won't! Now just you
listen to me! You no sooner get 'ere and you 'ave me
come upstairs, you takes me on, and then, without not
so much as a by-your-leave, you turns me out again!
When the old couple were 'ere, 'ere in this very room
where you're standing now ...

GENTLEMAN (*without making a gesture—his hands folded
behind his back*): May I suggest you go back to your
work? The postman may have called.

[The CARETAKER stops talking as
though she were suddenly really
frightened. The GENTLEMAN, motion-
less, stares at her, then he goes back
to the vase to admire it. Taking ad-
vantage of the fact that the GENTLE-
MAN's back is turned, the CARETAKER
makes a dash for the door on the
right, muttering to herself.]

CARETAKER: The vase is a bit of all right! (*Then, having
reached the door, she cries in a louder voice*) A mother
of five kids! You won't 'ave me on a bit of string! I'll
go and see the hinspector, I will!

[As she turns to go out she bumps
into the 2nd FURNITURE MOVER, who
is just coming in.]

Watch where you're going! (*She goes out, still shouting*)
You won't 'ave me on! You won't 'ave me on!

[The GENTLEMAN turns to the newcomer.]

2nd MOVER: Good day, sir. I've come about your furniture,
sir.

GENTLEMAN: Ah, yes! Good morning. Thank you. Your
associate is here already.

2nd MOVER: Good, I'll go and help him. I see he's already
started bringing them up.

GENTLEMAN: Oh yes! He's already started bringing them
up.

2nd MOVER: Has he been here long?

GENTLEMAN: No, only a few minutes.

2nd MOVER: Is there much left?

GENTLEMAN: Quite a lot, yes.

[Noises off on the other side.]

He's coming up now.

1st MOVER (*Off*): Are you there, Fred? Come and give me
a hand, will you?

[The 2nd MOVER goes off left, disappears for a moment and then can
just be seen coming in again backwards and straining hard. Meanwhile
the GENTLEMAN holds out his arm to
indicate different places in the room,
pointing to the floor, walls, and so on,
as though it were helping him to
imagine the arrangement of the
furniture.]

95

GENTLEMAN: One ... two ... three ... four ... one ...

1st MOVER (*Off*): That's it ... go ahead now!

GENTLEMAN (*as before*): One ... two ... three ... four ... one ...

> [Both FURNITURE MOVERS are now visible, struggling to carry between them another empty vase identical with the first and obviously extremely light in weight But their united effort should appear tremendous, so much so that they are in fact stumbling under their burden.]

1st MOVER: Come on now—once more! ...

2nd MOVER: Keep a good grip on it, there! ...

GENTLEMAN (*as before*): One ... two ... three ...

1st MOVER (*to* GENTLEMAN): Where's this one got to go?

GENTLEMAN: Let's see ... yes, put it there, please. That's it!

> [The FURNITURE MOVERS have put the vase down, as indicated, on a spot near the footlights, on the left. They straighten up, rubbing their arms and their backs, taking off their caps to wipe their foreheads. Meanwhile, the CARETAKER's voice can be heard from time to time raised in conversation and mixed up with other VOICES, but all the noise will subside gradually.]

2nd MOVER: Well, I hope everything's not going to be like that!

GENTLEMAN: Are you tired, gentlemen?

1st MOVER: Oh, it's nothing ... we're used to it, you

know. (*To his colleague*) Mustn't waste time! Shall we
go?

> [They both go out through the first
> door while the GENTLEMAN starts
> counting again.]

GENTLEMAN: One ... two ... three ... four ...

> [He is moving about choosing the
> places to put things and sometimes
> using the tape-measure.]

There, that will be fine ... and we can put that there
... and that can go here ... That's it ...

> [The 1st MOVER comes in carrying
> another vase, this time by himself
> but still with difficulty. The GENTLE-
> MAN points towards the other side of
> the stage, to the right-hand corner at
> the back, then goes on measuring.]

GENTLEMAN: One ... two ... three ... five ... one ... two
... seven ... Good ... that's it ... that'll be fine ...

1st MOVER: Is that where you want it, sir?

> [The larger and heavier the articles
> that the FURNITURE MOVERS bring on,
> the easier they seem to carry them
> until finally it looks like child's play.]

GENTLEMAN: Yes, that will do nicely.

> [The 1st MOVER goes off while the
> 2nd MOVER comes in through the
> same door, carrying another vase
> exactly like the rest.]

Will you put it there, please?

> [He points to right-hand corner near
> the footlights.]

2nd MOVER: Ah, yes!

> [He puts it down and goes off while
> the 1st MOVER comes in through the
> same door carrying two more tiny
> stools, exactly like the first ones and
> still with great effort.]

1st MOVER: And where are these to go, sir?

GENTLEMAN (*pointing either side of the opposite door*):
There and there, of course; then they'll match the
other side.

1st MOVER: Of course, I should have thought ... Phew!
Is there still any room left?

GENTLEMAN: There'll be enough. There's sure to be
enough. I have it all worked out.

> [The 1st MOVER goes off. The 2nd
> MOVER enters with a suitcase].

Put it there please ...

> [He points right of the window at
> back. Then changes his mind.]

I'm sorry. Not there. There ...

> [He points to the left of the window.]

2nd MOVER: Right, sir. It would help if you could be a
little more definite sir.

GENTLEMAN: Why yes, of course.

2nd MOVER: And then we won't tire ourselves out un-
necessarily.

GENTLEMAN: Of course, I understand.

> [The 1st MOVER enters with a pedestal
> table while the 2nd MOVER goes out.]

1st MOVER: Where shall I put this?

GENTLEMAN: Ah yes ... let me see ... it's not easy to find
the right little place for that ...

1st MOVER: Here, perhaps, sir! (*carries it to left of window*).

GENTLEMAN: The ideal place! Ideal!

[The 2nd MOVER comes in with another pedestal table. These tables are all in different shapes and colours.]

2nd MOVER: And this?

GENTLEMAN (*indicating place*): Here, if you don't mind.

2nd MOVER (*puts it down*): But there won't be any room for your plates!

GENTLEMAN: Everything's been accounted for.

2nd MOVER (*looking round stage*): I don't quite see ...

GENTLEMAN: Yes, I assure you.

2nd MOVER: Well, if you say so.

[He goes off, as the 1st MOVER arrives with another table.]

GENTLEMAN (*to 1st MOVER*): Beside the last one.

[While the 1st MOVER places the table in position and goes out, and the 2nd MOVER comes in with yet another table, the GENTLEMAN traces a circle on the floor in chalk, then more carefully, a large circle in the middle of the stage. He stops to show the 2nd MOVER where to put his latest pedestal table.]

There, along by the wall, next to the other! That will be fine!

[While the 2nd MOVER goes off the 1st MOVER arrives with another pedestal table.]

99

Next to the last one!

[He points out the place. The 1st MOVER puts it down and goes OFF. The GENTLEMAN, alone for a moment, counts the pedestal tables.]

Yes ... that's it ... now we shall have to ...

The 2nd MOVER comes in from the right, this time, with another pedestal table.]

All round the room ...

[Then, from the left, the 1st MOVER, with the seventh pedestal table.]

All around ...

[Both FURNITURE MOVERS go off, the 1st on the left, to come on again from the right, the 2nd on the right, to come in again from the left, and they bring on more tables and other objects such as chairs, screens, table-lamps, piles of books, etc., which they set down one after the other, all round the stage and along the walls, meeting and passing each other as they do so.]

All around the room, all around ... all around.

[Then, when the walls are all lined with the first row of furniture, the GENTLEMAN says to the 1st MOVER, who comes in, empty-handed from the left,]

Now you can bring a step-ladder!

[The 1st MOVER goes out the way he
came in, the 2nd comes on from the
right.]

A step-ladder!

[The 2nd MOVER goes out the way he
came in. The GENTLEMAN is looking
round the walls and rubbing his
hands together.]

There now! Now it's beginning to take shape. It'll be a
comfortable sort of place. It won't be at all bad.

[The FURNITURE MOVERS come in from
either side, each from that opposite
to the one they went out. The GENTLE-
MAN indicates to the one coming from
the left the wall on the right and
vice-versa. He says nothing.]

1st MOVER: Right ho!
2nd MOVER: Right ho!

[They cross and place their ladders
against the walls indicated.]

GENTLEMAN: Leave the ladders there. You can bring in
the pictures now!

[As he moves towards the exit, the
2nd MOVER steps on one of the chalk
circles.]

Be careful there! Don't spoil my circle.
2nd MOVER: Oh yes! We'll try not to.
GENTLEMAN: Be careful!

[The 2nd MOVER goes out while the
1st enters from the opposite side with
a large painting representing the
head of a hideous old man.]

Be careful, be careful of my circles.

1st MOVER: I'll try. It's not easy when you're loaded ...

GENTLEMAN: Now hang the picture up ...

1st MOVER: Yes, sir.

> [He climbs a ladder and carefully hangs it. The 2nd MOVER enters from the opposite side, also carrying a large painting representing another hideous old man.]

GENTLEMAN: My ancestors. (*To* 2nd MOVER) Now go up the ladder and hang the picture.

2nd MOVER: It's not easy, with all your circles. Especially when we come to the heavy objects. We can't watch out for everything.

GENTLEMAN: Oh yes you can, if you really want to.

> [The GENTLEMAN picks up from amongst the various objects brought on the stage, a book or a box or some other still smaller object and takes it to the centre of the stage where he sets it down after having inspected it by raising it above his head. Meanwhile the WORKMEN are busy fixing the paintings carefully on the two walls. The GENTLEMAN could also adjust the position of some of the furniture slightly or retrace his chalk circles again. All this without a word spoken. A slight sound of hammers and other exterior noises can still be heard, but already transformed into music. The GENTLEMAN contemplates the paintings and the room in general

with an air of satisfaction. This all
takes some time, in silence. At last
the FURNITURE MOVERS come down
from their ladders, and go and put
them where there is still a little space,
as for example near the two doors.
Then they join the GENTLEMAN who
studies first one picture, then the
other.]

1st MOVER: All right?

GENTLEMAN: All right?

2nd MOVER: Looks all right to me.

GENTLEMAN (*inspecting the pictures*): They're firmly fixed.
(*Pause*) Bring in the heavy objects.

2nd MOVER: It's thirsty work! (*Mops his brow*).

GENTLEMAN: We must have the sideboard then.

[Both FURNITURE MOVERS go towards
the door on the right.]

(*Turns towards window*) One ... yes ... one here ...

[Before the FURNITURE MOVERS can
reach them, the two folding doors
open of themselves and a sideboard
slides on to stage, propelled by an
invisible force. The doors close again
and the MOVERS seize the sideboard
and glance towards the GENTLEMAN.]

BOTH MOVERS: Where?

GENTLEMAN (*his back to audience, hands extended towards
window*): But there, of course! ...

1st MOVER: You'll shut out all the light.

GENTLEMAN: There's electric light, isn't there?

[The 1st MOVER pushes the sideboard
against the window. It fails to block

103

it up completely; it is not high enough. The 2nd MOVER goes and switches on the ceiling light, takes hold of a picture representing a winter landscape, which has glided on to the stage by itself through the folding doors, and places it on top of the sideboard. This time the window is completely masked. The 1st MOVER opens the sideboard, takes a bottle out, takes a swig from it, passes it to the 2nd MOVER, who does the same, and then offers it to the GENTLEMAN.]

GENTLEMAN: No, thank you. I never touch it.

[Both MOVERS drink in turn, handing the bottle backwards and forwards, and looking at the blocked-up window.]

Much better like that.

[All three have their backs to the audience.]

1st MOVER (*with approval*): Ah ha!

2nd MOVER (*with approval*): Ah ha!

GENTLEMAN: It's not quite right. (*indicating picture*) I don't like it ... turn it round!

[They turn it round while the GENTLE-MAN watches them. Then they step away a little, pick up the bottle, take a swig each, and then go and stand on either side of the GENTLEMAN, and again gaze at the sideboard and the picture on top of it. Silence for several moments.]

I like it better like that.

1st MOVER: It's much nicer.

GENTLEMAN: Much nicer. More restrained.

2nd MOVER: Much nicer. More restrained.

GENTLEMAN: Ah, yes, it's very much nicer, more restrained.

1st MOVER: Ah yes ...

2nd MOVER: Ah yes ...

GENTLEMAN: You can't see anything now.

1st MOVER: Well, that's something.

[Silence.]

2nd MOVER (*turning the bottle neck downwards*): There isn't any more.

1st MOVER: The last drop.

2nd MOVER (*to the* GENTLEMAN): There isn't any more.

GENTLEMAN: I don't think so either.

[The 1st MOVER takes the bottle and puts it in the sideboard.]

Won't have any trouble from the neighbours now.

1st MOVER: Better for everybody.

2nd MOVER: Everybody will be happy.

GENTLEMAN: Everyone will be happy. (*Pause*) To work. Let's go on. My armchair.

1st MOVER: Where can we put it?

2nd MOVER: Where can we put it?

GENTLEMAN: In the circle. (*Points to circle in middle.*) You won't be able to spoil my circle any more.

1st MOVER: You'll be able to see it better.

GENTLEMAN: Will you go and fetch it?

[The 1st MOVER starts towards the door on the right.]

(*To* 2nd MOVER) Now for the heavy furniture in pink wood.

[As the 1st MOVER arrives at the door, the armchair glides on, pushed from behind. He takes hold of it. The 2nd MOVER goes towards the opposite door, as half of a huge wardrobe lying on its side appears. He seizes hold of it and pulls it into the room. All the movements have slowed down; from now on all the furniture comes on through the two doors alternately, propelled from behind. Each item half appears, the MOVERS pull it towards them and when it has been pulled right into the room, something else slides on, half visible, and so on.]

(*Looking at the pink wardrobe*) It's a beautiful pink, isn't it?

1st MOVER (*after placing armchair within circle*): Good armchair.

GENTLEMAN (*feeling the upholstery*): Yes, it's very soft. Well upholstered. (*to 1st MOVER*) Please don't stop bringing the things in.

[The 1st MOVER goes back to his door, where he finds a second pink wardrobe on its side. The 2nd MOVER, still dragging his wardrobe on, glances at the GENTLEMAN.]

There!

[The wardrobes in question—there could be four in all—will be disposed, always according to the GENTLEMAN's directions, along the three walls,

parallel to the other rows of furniture.]

There! There! There! There!

[After the four wardrobes come
smaller items—some more tables,
settees too, wickerwork baskets,
strange furniture never seen before.
It is all placed in front of the rest
along the three walls, so that the
GENTLEMAN is confined in an ever-
diminishing space in the centre of
the stage. The action is like a ponder-
ous ballet and all the movements are
made very slowly. The GENTLEMAN is
in the centre with one hand on the
back of the armchair and the other
pointing.]

There ... there ... there ... there ... there ... there
... there ... there ... there ... there ...

[Then at a certain moment the 1st
FURNITURE MOVER brings on a radio
set, but when his questioning glance
alights on the GENTLEMAN, the latter
says in a voice scarcely louder than
before:]

Oh no! Oh dear me no!
1ST MOVER: It doesn't work.
GENTLEMAN: Well, in that case ... yes. Here.

[He indicates a spot near the armchair. Meanwhile the 2nd MOVER
comes up with the same look of inter-
rogation, carrying a chamber pot.]

Why yes, of course ... here.

> [He points to the other side of the
> armchair. Now the action continues
> in complete silence. Little by little
> the sounds from outside, the CARE-
> TAKER's voice, etc., have died away.
> The FURNITURE MOVERS pad about
> noiselessly, the furniture appears on
> the stage quite silently. Each time
> the FURNITURE MOVERS introduce a
> new item they still look questioningly
> at the GENTLEMAN and the latter still
> indicates by gesture, without uttering
> a word, where to put the various
> articles, which are slowly but surely
> closing in on him. Finally the 2nd
> MOVER brings on an enormous wall-
> clock. When the GENTLEMAN sees it,
> he shows surprise and uncertainty,
> then finally makes a sign of refusal.
> While the 2nd MOVER takes it away,
> the 1st MOVER arrives with a second
> clock that resembles the first in every
> respect. The GENTLEMAN dismisses him
> likewise, then changes his mind.]

But wait ... after all, why not?

> [Next the 2nd MOVER comes back
> with a large and very high screen. As
> he reaches the armchair the 1st
> MOVER comes up from his side also
> carrying a screen of the same height.]

2nd MOVER: There'll be no room left!
GENTLEMAN: Oh yes, there will. Like this there will.

[He sits down in his armchair within the circle. The FURNITURE MOVERS bring up a second and a third screen and enclose the GENTLEMAN on three sides. Only that facing the audience remains open. The GENTLEMAN is sitting in the armchair with his hat on his head, facing front. On each side the FURNITURE MOVERS poke their heads round the screens to have a look at him.]

1st MOVER: All right? You comfortable now?

[The GENTLEMAN nods his head.]

It's good to feel at home.

2nd MOVER: You must have got tired. I should have a little rest.

GENTLEMAN: Don't stop, will you? ... Is there still much left?

[The FURNITURE MOVERS make their way, each to one of the two entrances. The folding doors are wide open, but the two openings are completely blocked and one can only see great wooden boards, green on the left, purple on the right, as high as the doors themselves, apparently the backs of tall, wide wardrobes. Synchronizing their movements, each man looks at the door in front of him, scratches his head, shrugs his shoulders, steps back amongst the furniture, and turns to gape at the other.]

1st MOVER: What shall we do?

2nd MOVER: What shall we do?

GENTLEMAN (*without moving*): Is there still much left? Isn't it finished yet?

[They make gestures of bewilderment to each other.]

Have you brought up *all* the furniture?

[He remains quite calm, not moving. But he can no longer see them.]

1st MOVER: It's really rather awkward, sir.

GENTLEMAN: What is?

2nd MOVER: The rest of the furniture's very big and the doors aren't.

1st MOVER: Can't get it in.

GENTLEMAN: What is it that's left?

1st MOVER: Wardrobes.

GENTLEMAN: The green and the purple ones?

2nd MOVER: Yes.

1st MOVER: And that's not all. There's more to come.

2nd MOVER: The staircase is jammed from top to bottom. Nobody can get up or down.

GENTLEMAN: The yard is cram-full too. So is the street.

1st MOVER: The traffic's come to a standstill in the town. Full of furniture.

2nd MOVER: At least you've nothing to complain about, sir. You've got somewhere to sit.

1st MOVER: Perhaps the tube's still running.

2nd MOVER: No, it isn't.

GENTLEMAN: No. All the underground lines are blocked.

2nd MOVER: Some furniture! It's cluttering up the whole country.

GENTLEMAN: The Thames has stopped flowing too. Dammed up. No more water.

1st MOVER: What can we do then, if we can't get any
   more in?

GENTLEMAN: It can't be left outside, because of the weather.

1st MOVER: Might be able to get it in through the attic.
   But then ... we'd have to break the ceiling in.

2nd MOVER: Not necessary. Modern house. Sliding ceiling.
   (*To the* GENTLEMAN) Did you know?

GENTLEMAN: No.

2nd MOVER: Well, there you are. It's easy. Just have to
   clap your hands. The ceiling opens.

GENTLEMAN (*from his armchair*): No ... I'm afraid of the
   rain on the furniture. It's new and easily spoilt.

2nd MOVER: No fear of that, sir. I know how it works.
   The ceiling opens and closes, opens and closes, just as
   you want.

1st MOVER: Come on then, perhaps we can ...

GENTLEMAN (*from his armchair*): Providing you close it
   again at once. No carelessness, mind.

1st MOVER: We won't forget. *I'm* on the job. (*To the* 2nd
   MOVER) Ready?

2nd MOVER: Yes.

1st MOVER (*to the* GENTLEMAN): All right?

GENTLEMAN: Right.

1st MOVER (*to the* 2nd MOVER): Go ahead.


   [The 2nd MOVER claps his hands.
   From the ceiling huge planks descend
   at the front of the stage, completely
   hiding from view the GENTLEMAN in
   his high-walled enclosure; a few could
   also come down on to the stage
   amongst the furniture. The new
   tenant is completely walled-in. Clam-
   bering over the furniture the 1st

III

> MOVER, after knocking three times
> without response on one of the screens
> at the side, makes his way, with a
> ladder, to the place where the planks
> have completed the enclosure. He
> holds in one hand a bunch of flowers
> that he tries to hide from the audi-
> ence. Silently he leans his ladder up
> against an end-plank. When he has
> reached the top he looks down into
> the enclosure, and calls out,]

That's it. sir. Everything in. Are you nice and comfortable? Has the move gone off to your satisfaction?

GENTLEMAN'S VOICE (*just as it has always been, slightly
muffled, that's all*): Ceiling. Close ceiling please.

1st MOVER (*from the top of the ladder to his mate*): He
wants you to close the ceiling. You forgot.

2nd MOVER (*in the same spot*): Oh yes. (*claps for the ceiling to close again*) There you are.

GENTLEMAN'S VOICE: Thank you.

1st MOVER (*on the ladder*): Ah well, you've got a good
sheltered spot there, you won't be cold ... Are you all
right?

GENTLEMAN'S VOICE (*after a silence*): All right.

1st MOVER: Hand me your hat, sir, it might worry you.

> [After a short pause, the GENTLEMAN's
> hat can be seen appearing from with-
> in the enclosure. He takes it and
> throws the flowers down inside.]

That's right. You'll be more comfortable like that. Here
are some flowers for you. (*to 2nd MOVER*) Is that all?

2nd MOVER: That's all.

1st MOVER: Good. (*To the GENTLEMAN*) We've brought

everything, sir, you're really at home now. (*Comes down off ladder*) We'll be off.

> [He leans the ladder against the wall or perhaps he can prop it up, gently, without making a noise, somewhere amongst the other objects that hem the GENTLEMAN in.]

(*To* 2nd MOVER) Come on.

> [They make their way blindly and tentatively, to the back of the stage towards invisible and problematical exits, heaven knows where. For the window is stopped up and through the open folding doors you can still see the violently coloured wood that blocks the way. The 1st MOVER stops a moment, and calls back.]

Is there anything you want?

> [Silence.]

2nd MOVER: Is there anything you want?

GENTLEMAN'S VOICE (*after a pause, not a movement on the stage*): Put out the light. (*Utter darkness*) Thank you.

*Curtain*

# The Oyster and the Pearl

*William Saroyan (1908-    )*

## Characters

Harry Van Dusen, a barber
Clay Larrabee, a boy with Saturday off from school
Vivian McCutcheon, a new school teacher
Clark Larrabee, Clay's father
Man, a writer
Roxanna Larrabee, Clay's sister
Greeley, Clay's pal
Judge Applegarth, a beachcomber
Wozzeck, a watch repairer
A Garage Attendant

The Oyster and the Pearl

William Saroyan (1953)

# EDITOR'S NOTE

William Saroyan, one of America's best-known writers, offers a marked contrast to the other, and much younger, American represented in this volume, Edward Albee. Saroyan's plays and novels are famous for their at present rather unfashionable virtues of kindly optimism and faith in people. Certainly these are the qualities at the heart of *The Oyster and the Pearl.* They may strike some readers as a trifle sentimental—Saroyan is constantly being called that—but basically they are full of understanding for human foibles and not without a touch of worldly wisdom. When ours is so often thought of as an age which has no faith in anything, Saroyan points out in this play how some degree of faith is necessary to all of us if we are to keep going. Clay Larrabee believes there is a pearl in his oyster because he needs to believe it to make his world come right. Miss McCutcheon thinks it wrong not to acknowledge the truth and face facts, but Harry, who knows more about human nature, shows how a little faith, in its curious, roundabout way, can sometimes move mountains.

*The Oyster and the Pearl* was written for an American television series in 1953 (when Greeley mentions this year on p. 129 it should, of course, be brought up to date). But as, unlike most television plays, the action remains in one place, there is no difficulty in presenting it on a stage. No age is mentioned for Harry, but presumably he is one of those comfortable people who could be any age as long as it is not too young.

# THE OYSTER AND THE PEARL

SCENE: *Harry Van Dusen's barber shop in O.K.-by-the-Sea, California, population 909. The sign on the window says:* HARRY VAN DUSEN, BARBER. *It's an old-fashioned shop, crowded with stuff not usually found in barber shops ... Harry himself, for instance. He has never been known to put on a barber's white jacket or to work without a hat of some sort on his head: a stovepipe, a derby, a western, a homburg, a skull-cap, a beret, or a straw, as if putting on these various hats somewhat expressed the quality of his soul, or suggested the range of it.*

*On the walls, on shelves, are many odds and ends, some apparently washed up by the sea, which is a block down the street: abalone and other shells, rocks, pieces of driftwood, a life jacket, rope, sea plants. There is one old-fashioned chair.*

*When the play begins, Harry is seated in the chair. A boy of nine or ten named Clay Larrabee is giving him a haircut. Harry is reading a book, one of many in the shop.*

CLAY: Well, I did what you told me, Mr. Van Dusen. I hope it's all right. I'm not a barber, though. (*He begins to comb the hair.*)

HARRY: You just gave me a haircut, didn't you?

CLAY: I don't know *what* you'd call it. You want to look at it in the mirror? (*He holds out a small mirror.*)

HARRY: No thanks. I remember the last one.

CLAY: I guess I'll never be a barber.

117

HARRY: Maybe not. On the other hand, you may turn out
  to be the one man hidden away in the junk of the world
  who will bring merriment to the tired old human heart.

CLAY: Who? Me?

HARRY: Why not?

CLAY: Merriment to the tired old human heart? How do
  you do that?

HARRY: Compose a symphony, paint a picture, write a
  book, invent a philosophy.

CLAY: Not me! Did you ever do stuff like that?

HARRY: I did.

CLAY: What did you do?

HARRY: Invented a philosophy.

CLAY: What's that?

HARRY: A way to live.

CLAY: What way did you invent?

HARRY: The *Take-it-easy* way.

CLAY: Sounds pretty good.

HARRY: All philosophies sound good. The trouble with
  mine was, I kept forgetting to take it easy. Until one
  day. The day I came off the highway into this barber
  shop. The barber told me the shop was for sale. I told
  him all I had to my name was eighty dollars. He sold
  me the shop for seventy-five, and threw in the haircut.
  I've been here ever since. That was twenty-four years
  ago.

CLAY: Before I was born.

HARRY: Fifteen or sixteen years before you were born.

CLAY: How old were you then?

HARRY: Old enough to know a good thing when I saw it.

CLAY: What did you see?

HARRY: O.K.-by-the-Sea, and this shop—the proper place
  for me to stop. That's a couplet. Shakespeare had them
  at the end of a scene, so I guess that's the end of this

haircut. (*He gets out of the chair, goes to the hat tree, and puts on a derby.*)

CLAY: I guess I'd never get a haircut if you weren't in town, Mr. Van Dusen.

HARRY: Nobody would, since I'm the only barber.

CLAY: I mean, free of charge.

HARRY: I give you a haircut free of charge, you give me a haircut free of charge. That's fair and square.

CLAY: Yes, but you're a barber. You get a dollar a haircut.

HARRY: Now and then I do. Now and then I don't.

CLAY: Well, anyhow, thanks a lot. I guess I'll go down to the beach now and look for stuff.

HARRY: I'd go with you but I'm expecting a little Saturday business.

CLAY: This time I'm going to find something *real* good, I think.

HARRY: The sea washes up some pretty good things at that, doesn't it?

CLAY: It sure does, except money.

HARRY: What do you want with money?

CLAY: Things I need.

HARRY: What do you need?

CLAY: I want to get my father to come home again. I want to buy Mother a present ...

HARRY: Now, wait a minute, Clay, let me get this straight. Where *is* your father?

CLAY: I don't know. He went off the day after I got my last haircut, about a month ago.

HARRY: What do you mean, he went off?

CLAY: He just picked up and went off.

HARRY: Did he say when he was coming back?

CLAY: No. All he said was, Enough's enough. He wrote it on the kitchen wall.

HARRY: Enough's enough?

CLAY: Yeah. We all thought he'd be back in a day or two, but now we know we've got to *find* him and *bring* him back.

HARRY: How do you expect to do that?

CLAY: Well, we put an ad in *The O.K.-by-the-Sea Gull* ... that comes out every Saturday.

HARRY (*opening the paper*): This paper? But your father's not in town. How will he see an ad in this paper?

CLAY: He *might* see it. Anyhow, we don't know what else to do. We're living off the money we saved from the summer we worked, but there ain't much left.

HARRY: The summer you worked?

CLAY: Yeah. Summer before last, just before we moved here, we picked cotton in Kern County. My father, my mother, and me.

HARRY (*indicating the paper*): What do you say in your ad?

CLAY (*looking at it*): Well, I say ... Clark Larrabee. Come home. Your fishing tackle's in the closet safe and sound. The fishing's good, plenty of cabazon, perch, and bass. Let bygones be bygones. We miss you. Mama, Clay, Roxanna, Rufus, Clara.

HARRY: That's a good ad.

CLAY: Do you think if my father reads it, he'll come home?

HARRY: I don't know, Clay. I hope so.

CLAY: Yeah. Thanks a lot for the haircut, Mr. Van Dusen.

CLAY *goes out.* HARRY *takes off the derby, lathers his face, and begins to shave with a straight-edge razor. A pretty girl in a swimming suit comes into the shop, closing a colourful parasol. She has long blonde hair.*

HARRY: Miss America, I presume.

THE GIRL: Miss McCutcheon.

HARRY: Harry Van Dusen.

THE GIRL: How do you do.

HARRY (*bowing*): Miss McCutcheon.

THE GIRL: I'm new here.

HARRY: You'd be new anywhere—brand new, I might say. Surely you don't live here.

THE GIRL: As a matter of fact, I do. At any rate, I've been here since last Sunday. You see, I'm the new teacher at the school.

HARRY: You are?

THE GIRL: Yes, I am.

HARRY: How do you like it?

THE GIRL: One week at this school has knocked me for a loop. As a matter of fact, I want to quit and go home to San Francisco. At the same time I have a feeling I ought to stay. What do you think?

HARRY: Are you serious? I mean, in asking me?

THE GIRL: Of course I'm serious. You've been here a long time. You know everybody in town. Shall I go, or shall I stay?

HARRY: Depends on what you're looking for. I stopped here twenty-four years ago because I decided I wasn't looking for anything any more. Well, I was mistaken. I *was* looking, and I've found exactly what I was looking for.

THE GIRL: What's that?

HARRY: A chance to take my time. That's why I'm still here. What are *you* looking for, Miss McCutcheon?

THE GIRL: Well ...

HARRY: I mean, besides a husband ...

THE GIRL: I'm not looking for a husband. I expect a husband to look for me.

HARRY: That's fair.

THE GIRL: I'm looking for a chance to teach.

HARRY: That's fair too.

THE GIRL: But this town! ... The children just don't seem to care about anything—whether they get good grades or bad, whether they pass or fail, or anything else. On top of that, almost all of them are unruly. The only thing they seem to be interested in is games, and the sea. That's why I'm on my way to the beach now. I thought if I could watch them on a Saturday I might understand them better.

HARRY: Yes, that's a thought.

THE GIRL: Nobody seems to have any sensible ambition. It's all fun and play. How can I teach children like that? What can I teach them?

HARRY: English.

THE GIRL: Of course.

HARRY (*drying his face*): Singing, dancing, cooking ...

THE GIRL: Cooking? ... I must say I expected to see a much older man.

HARRY: Well! Thank you!

THE GIRL: Not at all.

HARRY: The question is, Shall you stay, or shall you go back to San Francisco?

THE GIRL: Yes.

HARRY: The answer is, Go back while the going's good.

THE GIRL: Why? I mean, a moment ago I believed you were going to point out why I ought to stay, and then suddenly you say I ought to go back. Why?

HARRY (*after a pause*): You're too good for a town like this.

THE GIRL: I am not!

HARRY: Too young and too intelligent. Youth and intelligence need excitement.

THE GIRL: There are *kinds* of excitement.

HARRY: Yes, there are. You need the big-city kind. There isn't an eligible bachelor in town.

THE GIRL: You seem to think all I want is to find a husband.

HARRY: But only to teach. You want to teach him to become a father, so you can have a lot of children of your own—to teach.

THE GIRL (*She sits almost angrily in the chair and speaks very softly*): I'd like a poodle haircut if you don't mind, Mr. Van Dusen.

HARRY: You'll have to get that in San Francisco, I'm afraid.

THE GIRL: Why? Aren't you a barber?

HARRY: I am.

THE GIRL: Well, this is your shop. It's open for business. I'm a customer. I've got money. I want a poodle haircut.

HARRY: I don't know how to give a poodle haircut, but even if I knew how, I wouldn't do it.

THE GIRL: Why not?

HARRY: I don't give women haircuts. The only women who visit this shop bring their small children for haircuts.

THE GIRL: I want a poodle haircut, Mr. Van Dusen.

HARRY: I'm sorry, Miss McCutcheon. In my sleep, in a nightmare, I would *not* cut your hair. (*The sound of a truck stopping is heard from across the street.*)

THE GIRL (*softly, patiently, but firmly*): Mr. Van Dusen, I've decided to stay, and the first thing I've got to do is change my appearance. I don't fit into the scenery around here.

HARRY: Oh, I don't know—if I were a small boy going to school, I'd say you look just right.

THE GIRL: You're just like the children. They don't take me seriously, either. They think I'm nothing more than a pretty girl who is going to give up in despair and go home. If you give me a poodle haircut I'll look more— well, plain and simple. I plan to dress differently, too.

123

I'm determined to teach here. You've got to help me. Now, Mr. Van Dusen, the shears, please.

HARRY: I'm sorry, Miss McCutcheon. There's no need to change your *appearance* at all.

*Clark Larrabee comes into the shop.*

HARRY: You're next, Clark. (*Harry helps Miss McCutcheon out of the chair. She gives him an angry glance.*

THE GIRL (*whispering*): I won't forget this rudeness, Mr. Van Dusen.

HARRY (*also whispering*): Never whisper in O.K.-by-the-Sea. People misunderstand. (*Loudly*) Good day, Miss.

MISS MCCUTCHEON *opens her parasol with anger and leaves the shop.* CLARK LARRABEE *has scarcely noticed her. He stands looking at* HARRY's *junk on the shelves.*

HARRY: Well, Clark, I haven't seen you in a long time.

CLARK: I'm just passing through, Harry. Thought I might run into Clay here.

HARRY: He was here a little while ago.

CLARK: How is he?

HARRY: He's fine, Clark.

CLARK: I been working in Salinas. Got a ride down in a truck. It's across the street now at the gasoline station.

HARRY: You've been home, of course?

CLARK: No, I haven't.

HARRY: Oh?

CLARK (*after a slight pause*): I've left Fay, Harry.

HARRY: You got time for a haircut, Clark?

CLARK: No thanks, Harry. I've got to go back to Salinas on that truck across the street.

HARRY: Clay's somewhere on the beach.

CLARK (*handing Harry three ten-dollar bills*): Give him this, will you? Thirty dollars. Don't tell him I gave it to you.

HARRY: Why not?

CLARK: I'd rather he didn't know I was around. Is he all right?

HARRY: Sure, Clark. They're *all* O.K. I mean ...

CLARK: Tell him to take the money home to his mother. (*He picks up the newspaper,* The Gull.)

HARRY: Sure, Clark. It came out this morning. Take it along.

CLARK: Thanks. (*He puts the paper in his pocket.*) How've things been going with *you,* Harry?

HARRY: Oh, I can't kick. Two or three haircuts a day. A lot of time to read. A few laughs. A few surprises. The sea. The fishing. It's a good life.

CLARK: Keep an eye on Clay, will you? I mean—well, I *had* to do it.

HARRY: Sure.

CLARK: Yeah, well ... That's the first money I've been able to save. When I make some more, I'd like to send it here, so you can hand it to Clay, to take home.

HARRY: Anything you say, Clark. (*There is the sound of the truck's horn blowing.*)

CLARK: Well ... (*He goes to the door.*) Thanks, Harry, thanks a lot.

HARRY: Good seeing you, Clark.

CLARK LARRABEE *goes out.* HARRY *watches him. A truck shifting gears is heard, and then the sound of the truck driving off.* HARRY *picks up a book, changes hats, sits down in the chair and begins to read. A man of forty or so, well-dressed, rather swift, comes in.*

THE MAN: Where's the barber?

HARRY: I'm the barber.

THE MAN: Can I get a haircut, real quick?

HARRY (*getting out of the chair*): Depends on what you mean by real quick.

THE MAN (*sitting down*): Well, just a haircut, then.

HARRY (*putting an apron around the man*): O.K. I don't believe I've seen you before.

THE MAN: No. They're changing the oil in my car across the street. Thought I'd step in here and get a haircut. Get it out of the way before I get to Hollywood. How many miles is it?

HARRY: About two hundred straight down the highway. You can't miss it.

THE MAN: What town is *this*?

HARRY: O.K.-by-the-Sea.

THE MAN: What do the people do here?

HARRY: Well, I cut hair. Friend of mine named Wozzeck repairs watches, radios, alarm clocks, and sells jewellery.

THE MAN: Who does he sell it to?

HARRY: The people here. It's imitation stuff mainly.

THE MAN: Factory here? Farms? Fishing?

HARRY: No. Just the few stores on the highway, the houses further back in the hills, the church, and the school. You a salesman?

THE MAN: No, I'm a writer.

HARRY: What do you write?

THE MAN: A little bit of everything. How about the haircut?

HARRY: You got to be in Hollywood tonight?

THE MAN: I don't have to be anywhere tonight, but that was the idea. Why?

HARRY: Well, I've alyways said a writer could step into a place like this, watch things a little while, and get a whole book out of it, or a play.

THE MAN: Or if he was a poet, a sonnet.

HARRY: Do you like Shakespeare's?

THE MAN: They're just about the best in English.

HARRY: It's not often I get a writer in here. As a matter of fact you're the only writer I've had in here in twenty years, not counting Fenton.

THE MAN: Who's he?

HARRY: Fenton Lockhart.

THE MAN: What's he write?

HARRY: He gets out the weekly paper. Writes the whole thing himself.

THE MAN: Yeah. Well ... How about the haircut?

HARRY: O.K.

HARRY *puts a hot towel around the man's head.* MISS MCCUTCHEON *carrying a cane chair without one leg and without a seat, comes in. With her is* CLAY *with something in his hand, a smaller boy named* GREELEY *with a bottle of sea water, and* ROXANNA *with an assortment of shells.*

CLAY: I got an oyster here, Mr. Van Dusen.

GREELEY: Miss McCutcheon claims there *ain't* a big pearl in it.

HARRY (*looking at* MISS MCCUTCHEON): Is she willing to admit there's a *little* one in it?

GREELEY: I don't know. I know I got sea water in this bottle.

MISS MCCUTCHEON: Mr. Van Dusen, Clay Larrabee seems to believe there's a pearl in this oyster he happens to have found on the beach.

CLAY: I didn't *happen* to find it. I went looking for it. You know Black Rock, Mr. Van Dusen? Well, the tide hardly ever gets low enough for a fellow to get around to the ocean side of Black Rock, but a little while ago it did, so I went around there to that side. I got to poking around and I found this oyster.

127

HARRY: I've been here twenty-four years, Clay, and this is the first time I've ever heard of anybody finding an oyster on our beach—at Black Rock, or anywhere else.

CLAY: Well, *I did*, Mr. Van Dusen. It's shut tight, it's alive, and there's a pearl in it, worth at least three hundred dollars.

GREELEY: A *big* pearl.

MISS MCCUTCHEON: Now, you children listen to me. It's never too soon for any of us to face the truth, which is supposed to set us free, not imprison us. The truth is, Clay, you want money because you need money. The truth is also that you have found an oyster. The truth is also that there is no pearl in the oyster.

GREELEY: How do you know? Did you look?

MISS MCCUTCHEON: No, but neither did Clay, and inasmuch as only one oyster in a million has a pearl in it, truth favours the probability that this is not the millionth oyster ... the oyster with the pearl in it.

CLAY: There's a *big* pearl in the oyster.

MISS MCCUTCHEON: Mr. Van Dusen, shall we open the oyster and show Clay and his sister Roxanna and their friend Greeley that there is no pearl in it?

HARRY: In a moment, Miss McCutcheon. And what's that *you* have?

MISS MCCUTCHEON: A chair, as you see.

HARRY: How many legs does it have?

MISS MCCUTCHEON: Three of course. I can count to three, I hope.

HARRY: What do you want with a chair with only three legs?

MISS MCCUTCHEON: I'm going to bring things from the sea the same as everybody else in town.

HARRY: But everybody else in town *doesn't* bring things

from the sea—just the children, Judge Applegarth, Fenton Lockhart, and myself.

MISS MCCUTCHEON: In any case, the same as the children, Judge Applegarth, Fenton Lockhart, and you. Judge Applegarth? Who's he?

HARRY: He judged swine at a county fair one time, so we call him Judge.

MISS MCCUTCHEON: Pigs?

HARRY: Swine's a little old-fashioned but I prefer it to pigs, and since both mean the same thing—Well, I wouldn't care to call a man like Arthur Applegarth a pig judge.

MISS MUCCUTCHEON: Did he actually judge swine, as you prefer to put it, at a county fair—one time? Did he even do *that*?

HARRY: Nobody checked up. He *said* he did.

MISS MCCUTCHEON: So that entitled him to be called Judge Applegarth?

HARRY: It certainly did.

MISS MCCUTCHEON: On that basis, Clay's oyster has a big pearl in it because he *says* so, is that it?

HARRY: I didn't say that.

MISS MCCUTCHEON: Are we living in the Middle Ages, Mr. Van Dusen?

GREELEY: No, this is 1953, Miss McCutcheon.

MISS MCCUTCHEON: Yes, Greeley, and to illustrate what I mean, that's water you have in that bottle. Nothing else.

GREELEY: *Sea* water.

MISS MCCUTCHEON: Yes, but there's nothing else in the bottle.

GREELEY: No, but there's little things in *the water*. You can't see them now, but they'll show up later. The water of the sea is full of things.

MISS MCCUTCHEON: Salt, perhaps.

129

GREELEY: No. *Living* things. If I look hard I can see some of them now.

MISS MCCUTCHEON: You can *imagine* seeing them. Mr. Van Dusen, are you going to help me or not?

HARRY: What do you want me to do?

MISS MCCUTCHEON: Open the oyster of course, so Clay will see for himself that there's no pearl in it. So he'll begin to face reality, as he should, as each of us should.

HARRY: Clay, do you mind if I look at the oyster a minute?

CLAY (*handing the oyster to* HARRY): There's a big pearl in it, Mr. Van Dusen.

HARRY (*examining the oyster*): Clay ... Roxanna ... Greeley ... I wonder if you'd go down the street to Wozzeck's. Tell him to come here the first chance he gets. I'd rather *he* opened this oyster. I might damage the pearl.

CLAY, GREELEY, *and* ROXANNA: O.K., Mr. Van Dusen. (*They go out.*)

MISS MCCUTCHEON: What pearl? What in the world do you think you're trying to do to the minds of these children? How am I ever going to teach them the principles of truth with an influence like yours to fight against?

HARRY: Miss McCutcheon. The people of O.K.-by-the-Sea are all poor. Most of them can't afford to pay for the haircuts I give them. There's no excuse for this town at all, but the sea is here, and so are the hills. A few people find jobs a couple of months every year North or South, come back half dead of homesickness, and live on next to nothing the rest of the year. A few get pensions. Every family has a garden and a few chickens, and they make a few dollars selling vegetables and eggs. In a town of almost a thousand people there isn't one rich man. Not even one who is well-off. And yet these people are the richest I have ever known. Clay doesn't really want money, as you seem to think. He wants his father to come home, and he thinks money will help get his father home. As a matter of fact his father is the man who stepped in here just as you were leaving. He left thirty dollars for me to give to Clay, to take home. His father and his mother haven't been getting along. Clark Larrabee's a fine man. He's not the town drunk or anything like that, but having four kids to provide for he gets to feeling ashamed of the showing he's making, and he starts drinking. He wants his kids to live in a good house of their own, wear good clothes, and all the other things fathers have always wanted for their kids. His wife wants these things for the kids, too. They don't have these things, so they fight. They had one too many fights about a month ago, so Clark went off—he's working in Salinas. He's either going to keep moving away from his family, or he's going to come back. It all depends on—well, I don't know what. This oyster maybe. Clay maybe. (*softly*) You and me maybe. (*There is a pause. He looks at the oyster. Miss McCutcheon looks at it, too.*) Clay believes there's a pearl in this oyster for the same reason you and I believe whatever *we* believe to keep *us* going.

MISS MCCUTCHEON: Are you suggesting we play a trick on Clay, in order to carry out your mumbo-jumbo ideas?

HARRY: Well, maybe it *is* a trick. I know Wozzeck's got a few pretty good-sized cultivated pearls.

MISS MCCUTCHEON: You plan to have Wozzeck pretend he has found a pearl in the oyster when he opens it, is that it?

HARRY: I plan to get three hundred dollars to Clay.

MISS MCCUTCHEON: Do you *have* three hundred dollars?

HARRY: Not quite.

MISS MCCUTCHEON: What about the other children who need money? Do you plan to put pearls in oysters for

them, too? Not just here in O.K.-by-the-Sea. Every-
where. This isn't the only town in the world where
people are poor, where fathers and mothers fight, where
families break up.

HARRY: No, it isn't, but it's the only town where I live.

MISS MCCUTCHEON: *I* give up. What do you want me to do?

HARRY: Well, could you find it in your heart to be just a
little less sure about things when you talk to the kids—
I mean, the troubled ones? You can get Clay around to
the truth easy enough just as soon as he gets his father
home.

*Arthur Applegarth comes in.*

HARRY: Judge Applegarth, may I present Miss McCutcheon?

THE JUDGE (*removing his hat and bowing low*): An honour,
Miss.

MISS MCCUTCHEON: How do you do, Judge.

HARRY: Miss McCutcheon's the new teacher at the school.

THE JUDGE: We are honoured to have you. The children,
the parents, and—the rest of us.

MISS MCCUTCHEON: Thank you, Judge. (*To* HARRY, *whispering*) I'll be back as soon as I change my clothes.

HARRY (*whispering*): I told you not to whisper.

MISS MCCUTCHEON (*whispering*): I shall expect you to give
me a poodle haircut.

HARRY (*whispering*): Are you out of your mind?

MISS MCCUTCHEON (*aloud*): Good day, Judge.

THE JUDGE (*bowing*): Good day, Miss. (*While he is bent
over he takes a good look at her knees, calves, ankles,
and bow-tied sandals.* MISS MCCUTCHEON *goes out. Judge
Applegarth looks from the door to* HARRY.

THE JUDGE: She won't last a month.

HARRY: Why not?

THE JUDGE: Too pretty. Our school needs an old battle-axe, like the teachers we had when we went to school, not a bathing beauty. Well, Harry, what's new?

HARRY: Just the teacher, I guess.

THE JUDGE: You know, Harry, the beach isn't what it used to be—not at all. I don't mind the competition we're getting from the kids. It's just that the quality of the stuff the sea's washing up isn't good any more. (*He goes to the door.*)

HARRY: I don't know. Clay Larrabee found an oyster this morning.

THE JUDGE: He did? Well, one oyster don't make a stew, Harry. On my way home I'll drop in and let you see what I find.

HARRY: O.K., Judge. (THE JUDGE *goes out.* HARRY *comes to life suddenly and becomes businesslike.*) Now, for the haircut! (*He removes the towel he had wrapped around the writer's head.*)

THE WRITER: Take your time.

HARRY (*He examines the shears, clippers, and combs*): Let's see now. (*The writer turns and watches. A garage attendant comes to the door.*)

THE ATTENDANT (*to the writer*): Just wanted to say your car's ready now.

THE WRITER: Thanks. (*The attendant goes out.*) Look. I'll tell you what. How much is a haircut?

HARRY: Well, the regular price is a dollar. It's too much for a haircut, though, so I generally take a half or a quarter.

THE WRITER (*getting out of the chair*): I've changed my mind. I don't want a haircut after all, but here's a dollar just the same. (*He hands* HARRY *a dollar, and he himself removes the apron.*)

HARRY: It won't take a minute.

THE WRITER: I know.

HARRY: You don't have to pay me a dollar for a hot towel. My compliments.

THE WRITER: That's O.K. (*He goes to the door.*)

HARRY: Well, take it easy now.

THE WRITER: Thanks. (*He stands for a moment, thinking, then turns.*) Do you mind if I have a look at that oyster?

HARRY: Not at all.

THE WRITER *goes to the shelf where* HARRY *has placed the oyster, picks it up, looks at it thoughtfully, puts it back without comment, but instead of leaving the shop he looks around at the stuff in it. He then sits down on a wicker chair in the corner, and lights a cigarette.*

THE WRITER: You know, they've got a gadget in New York now like a safety razor that anybody can give anybody else a haircut with.

HARRY: They have?

THE WRITER: Yeah, there was a full-page ad about it in last Sunday's *Times*.

HARRY: Is that where you were last Sunday?

THE WRITER: Yeah.

HARRY: You been doing a lot of driving.

THE WRITER: I like to drive. I don't know, though—those gadgets don't always work. They're asking two-ninety-five for it. You take a big family. The father could save a lot of money giving his kids a haircut.

HARRY: Sounds like a great idea.

THE WRITER: Question of effectiveness. If the father gives the boy a haircut the boy's ashamed of, well, that's not so good.

HARRY: No, a boy likes to get a professional-looking haircut all right.

THE WRITER: I thought I'd buy one, but I don't know.

HARRY: You got a big family?

THE WRITER: I mean for myself. But I don't know—there's something to be said for going to a barber shop once in a while. No use putting the barbers out of business.

HARRY: Sounds like a pretty good article, though.

THE WRITER (*getting up lazily*): Well, it's been nice talking to you. (WOZZECK, *carrying a satchel, comes in followed by* CLAY, ROXANNA, *and* GREELEY.)

WOZZECK: What's this all about Harry?

HARRY: I've got an oyster I want you to open.

ROXANNA: *He* doesn't believe there's a pearl in the oyster, either.

WOZZECK: Of course not! What foolishness!

CLAY: There's a *big* pearl in it.

WOZZECK: O.K., give me the oyster. I'll open it. Expert watch repairer, to open an oyster!

HARRY: How much is a big pearl worth, Louie?

WOZZECK: Oh, a hundred. Two hundred, maybe.

HARRY: A very *big* one?

WOZZECK: Three, maybe.

THE WRITER: I've looked at that oyster, and I'd like to buy it. (*To* CLAY) How much do you want for it?

CLAY: I don't know.

THE WRITER: How about three hundred?

GREELEY: Three hundred dollars?

CLAY: Is it all right, Mr. Van Dusen?

HARRY (*He looks at the writer, who nods*): Sure it's all right.

(THE WRITER *hands* CLAY *the money*.)

CLAY (*looking at the money and then at* THE WRITER): But suppose there ain't a pearl in it?

THE WRITER: There *is*, though.

WOZZECK: Don't you want to open it first?

THE WRITER: No, I want the whole thing. I don't think the pearl's stopped growing.

CLAY: He says there *is* a pearl in the oyster, Mr. Van Dusen.

HARRY: I think there is, too, Clay; so why don't you just go on home and give the money to your mother?

CLAY: Well ... I *knew* I was going to find something good today!

*The children go out.* WOZZECK *is bewildered.*

WOZZECK: Three hundred dollars! How do you know there's a pearl in it?

THE WRITER: As far as I'm concerned, the whole thing's a pearl.

WOZZECK (*a little confused*): Well, I got to get back to the shop, Harry.

HARRY: Thanks for coming by.

WOZZECK *goes out.* THE WRITER *holds the oyster in front of him as if it were an egg, and looks at it carefully, turning it in his fingers. As he is doing so,* CLARK LARRABEE *comes into the shop. He is holding the copy of the newspaper that* HARRY *gave him.*

CLARK: We were ten miles up the highway when I happened to see this classified ad in the paper. (*He hands the paper to* HARRY *and sits down in the chair.*) I'm going out to the house, after all. Just for the weekend of course, then back to work in Salinas again. Two or three months, I think I'll have enough to come back for a long time. Clay come by?

HARRY: No, I've got the money here.

CLARK: O.K., I'll take it out myself, but first let me have the works—shave, haircut, shampoo, massage.

HARRY (*putting an apron on* CLARK): Sure thing, Clark.

(*He bends the chair back, and begins to lather* CLARK's *face.* MISS MCCUTCHEON, *dressed neatly, looking like another person almost, comes in.*)

MISS MCCUTCHEON: Well?

HARRY: You look fine, Miss McCutcheon.

MISS MCCUTCHEON: I don't mean that. I mean the oyster.

HARRY: Oh, that! There *was* a pearl in it.

MISS MCCUTCHEON: I don't believe it.

HARRY: A *big* pearl.

MISS MCCUTCHEON: You might have done me the courtesy of waiting until I had come back before opening it.

HARRY: Couldn't wait.

MISS MCCUTCHEON: Well, I don't believe you, but I've come for my haircut. I'll sit down and wait my turn.

HARRY: Mr. Larrabee wants the works. You'll have to wait a long time.

MISS MCCUTCHEON: Mr. Larrabee? Clay's father? Roxanna's father? (CLARK *sits up.*)

HARRY: Clark, I'd like you to meet our new teacher, Miss McCutcheon.

CLARK: How do you do.

MISS MCCUTCHEON: How do you do, Mr. Larrabee. (*She looks bewildered.*) Well, perhaps some other time, then, Mr. Van Dusen. (*She goes out.* CLARK *sits back.* JUDGE APPLEGARTH *stops at the doorway of the shop.*)

THE JUDGE: Not one thing on the beach, Harry. Not a blessed thing worth picking up and taking home. (JUDGE APPLEGARTH *goes on.* THE WRITER *looks at* HARRY.)

HARRY: See what I mean?

THE WRITER: Yeah. Well ... so long. (*He puts the oyster in his coat pocket.*)

HARRY: Drop in again any time you're driving to Hollywood.

THE WRITER: Or away. (*He goes out.*)

CLARK (*after a moment*): You know, Harry, that boy of mine, Clay ... well, a fellow like that, you can't just go off and leave him.

HARRY: Of course you can't Clark.

CLARK: I'm taking him fishing tomorrow morning. How about going along, Harry?

HARRY: Sure, Clark. Be like old times again. (*There is a pause.*)

CLARK: What's all this about an oyster and a pearl?

HARRY: Oh, just having a little fun with the new teacher. You know, she came in here and asked me to give her a poodle haircut? A poodle haircut! I don't believe I remember what a poodle *dog* looks like, even.

# The Interview

*J. P. Donleavy (1926-    )*

## Characters

Stephen Mott
Cornelius Christian
Howard How
Miss Kelly

# EDITOR'S NOTE

*The Interview* is actually the second of four independent episodes, linked only by the central character, Cornelius Christian, which together make up a full-length play called *Fairy Tales of New York*. The name Christian recalls the hero of Bunyan's *Pilgrim's Progress*, and *Fairy Tales of New York* is really a sort of satirical pilgrim's progress through modern America. Cornelius, one gathers, is himself an American, but he has spent impressionable years in Europe and now tends to talk with an English accent (J. P. Donleavy, too, was born in New York but now lives in London). And he comes back to his homeland blandly applying Old World values to the New and unsettling everyone he comes across by behaving as a non-conformist in a society strictly ruled by convention. In this episode we see him tangling with the traditional American world of big business (with its senior and junior executives, its talk of efficiency and the power of salesmanship, its worship of success, and all the other clichés of the 'organization men') and by sheer innocence winning through. Perhaps the play could be called, like the popular American musical, 'How To Succeed in Business Without Really Trying'.

Donleavy writes with an original, dry style of humour (notice the highly individual stage-directions), but like many of today's younger dramatists, he also possesses an exceptionally acute ear for authentic dialogue. He catches (and caricatures) exactly the way certain Americans talk. The play was originally presented in London on an arena-stage—that is to say, an open acting-area which has the audience sitting round three sides of it—and it probably works better done like this than on a conventional stage with curtains and scenery. All that is needed are two desks, a sofa and some chairs, with lighting that shifts from one area to the other to indicate the different rooms. The windows can be suggested through mime.

# THE INTERVIEW

SCENE I

*New York. Mott's office.*
*An April morning:* STEPHEN MOTT *leans over and speaks into his desk microphone.*

MOTT: Send in Mr. Christian.

CORNELIUS CHRISTIAN *collegiately crossing to take* MOTT'S *outstretched hand.*

Well, if it isn't my boy Christian, isn't it?

CHRISTIAN: Yes, Mr. Mott, it is.

MOTT: Well, sit down, delighted to see you, son. Have a smoke, my boy?

CHRISTIAN: No, thanks.

MOTT: Well, what can I do for you?

CHRISTIAN: Mr. Mott, I'd like to make money.

MOTT: Ha, ha. Well that's pretty straightforward, you might say that it's a universal incentive. A word we use a lot around here, I mean incentive. Like that type of word, connotes purpose. Well now. How do you feel we can help? Got something to offer us?

CHRISTIAN: Myself.

MOTT: Well now, another pretty straightforward answer. I like that. It's Cornelius Christian, isn't it?

CHRISTIAN: Yes.

MOTT: Well now, I'll call you Cornelius. Well Cornelius, so you'd like to make money. Come over here.

CHRISTIAN *to window behind* MOTT.

Down there is the harbour of New York. Just look down there. What puts us way up here?

142

CHRISTIAN: Well I guess the elevator.

MOTT: Boy, I'm talking on a different level.

CHRISTIAN: Oh.

MOTT: Ingenuity. It's a word we use around here. Say it.

CHRISTIAN: Ingenuity.

MOTT: Come on, let's have some lung.

CHRISTIAN: Ingenuity.

MOTT: That's better, boy. I remember you. A party of my son's wasn't it? Couple of month's ago. Just back from Europe weren't you? I remember that party. The jukebox got short-circuited in the rumpus room. Remember a couple of comments you made caught my ear. Yeah.

CHRISTIAN: Yes, I was at the party.

MOTT: Look, tell you what. Bit rushed just now, excuse me a second. (*Into desk microphone*) Miss Peep, get me personal, Mr. How. (*The large smiles of friendliness in the pause*) Ah. Hello Howard. Got a young man here, friend of my boy's. He wants to make money. Want you to talk to him and show him around. Thinks we can use him. Yes. (*Turning to* CHRISTIAN) Cornelius, you free right now?

CHRISTIAN: Certainly, yes.

MOTT (*into desk microphone*): All right Howard, you take care of that. Kids, Howard, O.K.? Fine. Well, life will get less noisier as you get older, Howard, and the kids grow up. Great. Fine. Great. That's great. O.K. Howard. 'Bye. (*Turning to* CHRISTIAN) Well, Cornelius, our Mr. How will show you around. See what we can do. And he'll talk it over with you. Maybe we can have a chat again. I like to talk to the young kids coming along. Now what's that word.

CHRISTIAN: Ingenuity.

MOTT: 'at-a-boy, Christian.

CHRISTIAN: Thanks very much, Mr. Mott.

MOTT: Any time, Christian.

CHRISTIAN: And hope that spot's a little better. (MOTT *surprised*) You know the spot you had in front of your eyes, said you could follow it out the window like it was a bumble bee only it would always come back again.

MOTT: You got some memory boy.

*The long pause that does not refresh.*

And memory makes money. Remember that utterance. Words are wonderful. Remember that too.

CHRISTIAN: It's been extremely good of you, Mr. Mott.

MOTT: Anything anytime for the young people. Keep in touch. Find Mr. How five floors down.

CHRISTIAN: Thanks again, Mr. Mott.

MOTT's *smile.* CHRISTIAN *exits.* MOTT's *stone face.*

*Blackout*

SCENE II

*How's Office.*

HOWARD HOW *studiously at his desk.* CORNELIUS CHRISTIAN *entering.*

HOW: Mr. Christian?

CHRISTIAN: Yes.

HOW: I'm Howard How. (*Outstretched hand*)

CHRISTIAN: Hello. I'm thinking of moving to the Bronx.

(*His hand goes to lip, my, what an utterance*)

HOW: You're what?

CHRISTIAN: Oh, sorry, Mr. How. Guess I'm nervous. I've just strangely had something on my mind about the Bronx. Once it was meadow land, I've been reading an old guide book.

HOW: Oh?

CHRISTIAN: Yes, ha, ha. Was thinking maybe some parts might still be meadow land.

HOW: We manufacture spark plugs, Mr. Christian.

CHRISTIAN: Of course, of course. I don't dispute that for a minute.

HOW: And there are no meadows left in the Bronx.

CHRISTIAN: I would never dispute that either.

HOW: What do you dispute?

CHRISTIAN: I don't dispute anything. Nothing at all. Oh, there are some things I don't like, all right. But I don't dispute anything. It was just that when I was looking out of the train—(CHRISTIAN *upturns a left supplicant hand*)—I just thought once (*looking into hand*) there were real Indians running around here.

HOW: Well let's get back to the twentieth century now.

CHRISTIAN: Sure.

HOW: And you're interested in our using you.

CHRISTIAN: I'd like it if you could.

HOW: Point is, Mr. Christian, just what can we use you for. I note you have a rather English tone to your voice. Didn't by any chance pick that up in the Bronx?

CHRISTIAN: As a matter of fact I learned it out of a book.

HOW: Oh. Now look, I'm not trying to hurt your feelings. For what it's worth you might as well know Mr. Mott likes to have an English quality about the place. You've noticed the rural scenes of England in the halls. We know how to appreciate that kind of atmosphere here.

CHRISTIAN: Yes, nice and green. I mean, you know, rustic. I like it.

HOW: Glad. We feel it's a nice contrast to the product. Well, aesthetically we've made progress together. Arrived at a nice base to use as a springboard. Now. Well, what, Mr. Christian, are you exactly interested in doing. What are your qualifications, your degrees?

CHRISTIAN: Well, as a matter of fact, Mr. How—

HOW: Good. The facts. That's what we want, Christian, the facts.

CHRISTIAN (*quickly out with the handkerchief to deal with sudden nose tickling*): I just missed, I guess, by only a few subjects of course, getting my degree. At that time I had a lot of things on my mind. You see I've always been deeply interested in human nature and I guess I got distracted.

HOW: Sorry, Mr. Christian, but I understand you don't have a degree.

CHRISTIAN: Well. Except of misery I guess. (*The leaning forward. The careful agonization*) But I almost made it.

HOW: Don't be alarmed, Christian, these notes I'm making are just a few facts. Note you got alacrity with words.

CHRISTIAN: But I almost made it, I really did.

HOW: Easy, boy. Easy. We make spark plugs. We want to make money.

CHRISTIAN's *face the setting sun of sincerity.*

You know, I can see you really do, don't you?

CHRISTIAN: Yes.

HOW: I'm glad your desire is sincere.

CHRISTIAN: Thanks.

HOW: We have progressed. You're a friend of Mr. Mott's son, I presume. Mr. Mott's a friendly but very busy man and this affair more or less, you understand me, rests in my hands if we're going to find something for you. Do you have any preference as regards production or management?

CHRISTIAN: Well. I'd like to manage, if that can be arranged.

HOW: Just give that pitcher of water a push in my direction will you. Want some water?

CHRISTIAN: Thanks a lot. (*The good things are free*)

HOW: You got a far-away look in your eye.

CHRISTIAN: Well you see this water's got a history.

HOW: Oh.

CHRISTIAN: You'll think I'm crazy.

HOW: I'm prepared to wait until conclusions are conclusive. Let's hear the water's history.

CHRISTIAN: Well the water has got to come from the Catskills.

HOW: That's fairly common knowledge.

CHRISTIAN: From the Ashokan Reservoir.

HOW: Maybe that fact is not common.

CHRISTIAN: I read in a geography book as a kid what they had to do. Am I boring you?

HOW: Oh, no. I'm fascinated.

CHRISTIAN: Well, I know it's ridiculous but I just can't forget what it took to make this reservoir. Fifteen thousand acres. Seven villages sunk. Thirty-two cemeteries with two thousand eight hundred bodies they had to dig up.

HOW *pushing his glass away.*

And even an eighteen-mile tunnel through the mountains which is one of the longest subterranean aqueducts in the world.

HOW: Boy, you're just full of facts.

CHRISTIAN (*raising glass*): I guess we might be drinking somebody's soul.

HOW's *raised head to look towards sunnier thoughts.*

I'm glad I've had this drink of water. Thanks.

HOW: Don't mention it. (HOW's *licking of the lips*) We better reconstruct the relationship here. You're still looking for a job.

CHRISTIAN: Oh, yes.

HOW: O.K. We want men with ideas. Ideas more than anything. I may mention along this line that we prefer these ideas to be of a red-blooded nature as opposed to weird. Can you type?

CHRISTIAN: Well. My parents gave me one of those little typewriters when I was a kid but I don't expect that would qualify me as a typist at the moment, but it's something I could pick up. I pick up most things rather easily—

HOW: Like your degree, for instance.

CHRISTIAN: Look, Mr. How. I'm after a job. I don't want to misrepresent myself or give a false impression, but as I said I'm interested in human nature.

HOW: You said that.

CHRISTIAN: I don't have a degree. O.K. Maybe I was too distracted by human nature in college. I got disappointed in human nature as well and gave it up because I found it too much like my own.

HOW: Wow, Christian. You're some candidate.

CHRISTIAN: But I wasn't stupid, you know.

HOW: Look, Mr. Christian. You don't mind if we don't bother seeing things today. I mean you'll understand that until we know what you can do there isn't really much point in my showing you our set-up at the moment. I know Mr. Mott's one of the friendliest men you could ever want to meet and I know he wants to help you, but it is rather a question, in the end, can you help us?

CHRISTIAN: Yes, I understand.

HOW: You're a very presentable person and, of course, well spoken and, by the way, I like the way you tie your knots, that's a nice tie, always be sure of a man in this business if he wears a knitted tie. Just want us both to face the facts, Christian. Just the facts.

148

CHRISTIAN: O.K.

HOW: Got an opening for a courier representative. (*at papers*) Dispatch and deliver various important papers. Expenses, taxi, and all the rest.

CHRISTIAN: I'm almost thirty years old. You mean I deliver papers? Like a messenger boy?

HOW: Not in so many words, Mr. Christian. Not in so many words. It's of the nature of a confidential dispatch agent and you would, of course, hold the title of executive courier.

CHRISTIAN: What are the friends I've known all my life going to say. They'd be overjoyed. Never stop laughing. I went to college you know.

HOW: A lot, an awful lot of people go to college, Mr. Christian. Mr. Mott never went to college and he controls a business extending to twenty-nine states—we just added Texas yesterday.

CHRISTIAN: Well, I've had a job before.

HOW: I'm keeping an open mind. I'm perfectly reasonable you know, Mr. Christian. What sort of work did you do? You see I'm not here to bring about a stalemate with applicants. I'm here to hire the right man for the right job. O.K.? Now what exactly are you experienced in?

CHRISTIAN: Does it matter?

HOW: That's up to you. I'm only trying to help. Just testing your qualifications. Want to know the sort of work you're best suited for. Where your interests truly lie. We're an outfit you know, where, when it's expedient, we take off our jackets, you understand me, and roll up our sleeves. And being a courier executive would allow your capabilities to rise to the surface. You see what I mean?

CHRISTIAN: To be frank, I've been, well, I'm experienced.

HOW: O.K. But frank with the facts, Christian. How were you used?

CHRISTIAN: They used me, I guess as a sort of representative, as you might say. A specialist in human relations. As I've said I could count myself as a former student of human nature.

HOW: Yes, I know, you've said that three times now. You were in public relations then.

CHRISTIAN (*an abhorer of relations in public*): Well yes, sort of, I guess. I wasn't too clear at the time because I had a lot of things on my mind.

HOW: What firm was this?

CHRISTIAN: As a matter of fact—

HOW: That's right, the facts, Christian—

CHRISTIAN: It was called the Stars of the Forest, I guess, Incorporated.

HOW: How's that, boy?

CHRISTIAN: Stars of the Forest.

HOW: Don't mind telling me their product? Briefly.

CHRISTIAN: Death.

HOW: How's that, boy?

CHRISTIAN: Death.

HOW: What?

CHRISTIAN: What I'm telling you, death. One word.

HOW: You mean undertaker?

CHRISTIAN: Since we're down to one word, yes, an undertaker. A Mr. Vine, director, of Stars of the Forest, said I excelled in that professional capacity.

HOW: Well you know, God help me, Christian, I honestly don't know what to make of you. Get that chair over there and sit down. It's not been in my experience previous to this to consider anybody in the light, or, forgive me, darkness, of these circumstances. How long did you undertake?

CHRISTIAN: I undertook for, well, not long. I'm begging for a chance to prove myself, Mr. How. Just one chance.

HOW: Easy. Take it easy. (*hand to brow*) Just got to think. What an interview. I am deeply involved in this disorientation. Just let me ask you a question will you? Wait, excuse me a second. (*speaking into desk microphone*) Miss Kelly, would you please play over to me the background music we've chosen for Friday's conference for our Chicago representatives?

KELLY (*disembodied*): Yes, Mr. How.

*Tchaikovsky's Andante Cantabile for strings.*

HOW: Cornelius. Now look, tell me, were you looking for this job? Don't have to answer that if you don't want.

CHRISTIAN: Someone close to me died.

HOW: Sorry to hear that. By the way, you like this music?

CHRISTIAN: It's nice.

HOW: Soothes, doesn't it. Guess it's been one of the most successful innovations Mr. Mott introduced into business practice, almost like the invention of the wheel. (*Glum* CHRISTIAN) Come on, Cornelius, cheer up. Only thing is we got a problem here. Your job in the funeral parlour business is not going to cut much ice with Mr. Mott, in fact the mere mention of it will throw a distinct chill into him. But I'll tell you something before we go any further, you know, I like you, I think you're O.K.

CHRISTIAN: Thanks.

HOW: You know, most of the people sent along to me with pull with Mr. Mott aren't worth their weight in paper, strictly between us, you understand. You strike me as a guy with imagination. I'm going to give you a chance. If I assign you to our idea department, do you suppose

you could get some ideas. It'd be a trial, you understand.

CHRISTIAN: Ideas about what?

HOW: Come on, Cornelius, what am I letting myself in
for? Quick. Ideas. We make spark plugs. Mr Mott loves
the use of words. Think of something. Quick.

CHRISTIAN: My mind's a blank at the moment.

HOW (*into desk microphone*): Miss Kelly, give us something faster, for a fast idea session of approximately
forty-five seconds starting ten seconds from now.

KELLY (*without body*): Coming ten seconds from now.

CHRISTIAN: Gee, I'm worried. My whole life depends upon
what I might say.

HOW: Wouldn't put it like that. Think. One sentence.
One idea, a rhyme, anything, don't care what it is, so
long as it underlines an inescapable fact.

CHRISTIAN: But all my facts have escaped.

*Liszt's Hungarian Rhapsody.*

HOW: Go, go, boy.

CHRISTIAN: I can't go anywhere, Mr. How, I swear it. The
facts have escaped.

HOW: Go after them, boy. I know you can do it. Think of
something to do with a spark plug. Think of the money.
Money, boy. Think of the money.

CHRISTIAN: I am. Wait. If you've got a heart, you've got a
spark that could be a heart by Mott.

HOW *a giant in success.*

CHRISTIAN, *a sigh, a relaxing back.*

When you said money, those words just came pouring
into my mind.

HOW: Don't be ashamed of that, boy. (*Into microphone*)
Miss Kelly, good, it did the trick, neat selection, make
a note of it.

KELLY (*no body*): Glad it worked, Mr. How.

HOW: It was swell. And make a note, we've got a new man for our idea department starting right away.

KELLY (*bodyless*): Yes, indeed, Mr. How.

HOW (*standing, hand extended to* CHRISTIAN, *a glad hand*):

CHRISTIAN's *descent into deflation.*

Hey, boy. Hey, there.

CHRISTIAN (*comes to, jumps to take that glad hand*): Oh!

HOW: You're in. Boy.

CHRISTIAN: Mean I'm hired?

HOW: Of course.

CHRISTIAN: Just like that?

HOW: Just like that.

CHRISTIAN: Well, isn't it too quick? Isn't there something more? Can't I fill something out? I just don't feel it's me.

HOW: Cornelius, I think you've got what it takes. Yes, If you've got a heart, you've got a spark that could be a heart by Mott. Here, gee, have another drink of water. Yes. Ingenuity—

CHRISTIAN (*mouth coming up out of the water which displaced 2,800 dead bods*): —makes industry

HOW (*leaning over microphone*): Miss Kelly, can you hear what's happening in here?

KELLY (*vocal*): Yes, I can, Mr. How. It's wonderful.

HOW: Well, get it down.

KELLY: Got it, Mr. How.

HOW: Flash those two things to Mr. Mott. He's got to hear about this right away. Ingenuity makes industry. A follow-up to Mr. Mott's favourite word.

CHRISTIAN: But this is awful, I mean I feel overrated, just for a few words.

HOW (*looking down an index finger at the level of his*

*eye*): We find a guy, Cornelius, with words like that coming out of his head, we buy that head.

CHRISTIAN: Mr. How, I'm—I think I'd rather be a messenger boy.

HOW (*into desk microphone*): Miss Kelly, I want you to shout back just what you think of Christian's word formations.

KELLY: They're really impressive.

HOW: Now, boy, hear that?

CHRISTIAN: But I'll tell you the truth—

HOW *calmly waiting for truth.*

—no, maybe I better not.

HOW *smiling warmly.*

But I don't know a thing about spark plugs or industry. Except that there's money in it somewhere.

HOW: Isn't that enough, boy. Money is the moment of truth. Boy. You have saddened my life right now.

CHRISTIAN *sadder.*

(*Into desk microphone*) Miss Kelly, would you make a fresh statement. Just tell him. Exactly what you think.

KELLY (*without body*): I think he's really spontaneous.

HOW: There you are, boy.

CHRISTIAN: I'm only just a reasonably normal person.

HOW (*deep concern*): You're not normal, boy. I know it.

CHRISTIAN *coming alive.*

Oh, wait. Hold it. Whoa. Let's reconstruct this relationship here. (*Into desk microphone*) Miss Kelly would you see that Cornelius and myself are left undisturbed for a few minutes and stop all calls. We just need a little talk.

KELLY (*disembodied*): Certainly, Mr. How, anything for background music?

HOW: Not for the moment thanks. (*To* CHRISTIAN) Now look, Cornelius, let's sit over here. (*Side by side on leather sofa*) I'll give it to you straight. When Mr. Mott gets these messages he's going to want to see you right away. Now I'm going to risk my life. You know why? Because I like you. When you first came in here I just thought you were another snooty sophisticate out of the ivy leagues. But you know, you've got a real quality in you. Which goes deeper than shirt and tie.

CHRISTIAN: My job in the funeral parlour, I suppose. But it was the only thing I could get when I first got back from Europe.

HOW: That's what I want to talk about. It's Europe. That's the thing's given you this quality too. A sort of thing that's real. Breeding. But look. I've got absolute faith in you. You could dazzle this industry.

CHRISTIAN: Mr. How, thanks, but I think you're making a mistake. I'm not like that at all. That's just the way I appear. Some of the things I really think and believe would revolt you. I'm almost a criminal type.

HOW: What a remark. You're just full of ideas, boy. Why you're not more of a criminal than I am—(CHRISTIAN *alive*) I mean—(HOW's *light smile of relief*)—I just mean we're alike. But look. I'm maybe ten years older than you. Got wife, kids, nice home out in Long Island. The real things. Sure I've got some gripes. But I'll tell you something. See those binoculars. Want you to look out the window with them. Go ahead.

CHRISTIAN *to window with binoculars.*

Towards the Statue of Liberty. Got it? Now a little to the left.

CHRISTIAN: Yes.

HOW: See those barges?

CHRISTIAN: I think so.

HOW: That's refuse. Happens every day, all day. Come down the Hudson and out of East River, filled with stuff that's no more use. They dump it. Christian, it's made an awful impression on me. See, dumped. Maybe not in a river, but you know what I mean.

CHRISTIAN: Mr. How, I've lost my ambition.

HOW: Boy, don't ever say a thing like that. Not good for you to say it and it's not good for me to hear. Boy and I've heard an earful.

CHRISTIAN: But I mean it, Mr. How.

HOW: Call me Howard, Cornelius. As a personal favour I'm asking you right now to take this job. I know everything's going to click. Do it for me. You know, I've got to laugh, here I am begging you to work for us and ten minutes ago I was wondering how I was politely going to discourage you.

CHRISTIAN: Dump.

HOW: Well yeah, but—no, no—

KELLY (*without body*): Excuse me for interrupting, Mr. How, but Mr. Mott wants you to come up to his private reception room right away.

HOW: There, boy. (*Into microphone*) Thanks, Miss Kelly. Right. Now, Cornelius. I'm asking you now, please, I've got to go through with this now. Just be yourself. Just let your personality come out as it's done with me. Only just don't give any hint of your past employment. Mr. Mott's toleration for the suppression of facts is nil, but to me, it's worth the risk. Just go in with the trace of a smile, that's all I'm asking you.

CHRISTIAN'S *mumchance mumification.*

But don't look like that.

CHRISTIAN: I'm O.K., Mr. How.

*Softly, Beethoven music.*

My memory's just working.

HOW *touched. A long silence.*

HOW: Yeah. (*Sadness*) Anyway, just say that thing once more.

CHRISTIAN: You mean about industry?

HOW: Please. With conviction. Ingenuity makes—

CHRISTIAN: I think I've got something better. Ingenuity made Mott, Mott makes industry.

HOW: Miss Kelly, get something for my heart, it's missing beats and get this down, it's Christian again. Ingenuity made Mott, Mott makes industry.

KELLY (*no body*): Shall I flash that to Mr. Mott?

HOW: No, no. He's got a weak heart too.

*Black Out*

### SCENE III

MOTT'S PRIVATE RECEPTION ROOM.

*Large room.* MOTT *sits in low chair. Window behind. Table covered with phones at his elbow. Legs crossed. Holding up his hand for* CHRISTIAN *to shake.* CHRISTIAN *walks across and takes it.*

MOTT: Howard, you saw what I didn't see, at first sight that is.

HOW (*slight wringing of the hands*): It was nothing, Steve. Miss Kelly selected the background music.

MOTT: Sit over there, Christian. (*To a distant seat on his right*)

HOW *to a distant seat on* MOTT'S *left.*

Well, let's hear all these nice things.

157

HOW: Steve, he's got something even better, didn't want to flash it.

MOTT: Give us a flash now, Christian.

CHRISTIAN: Ingenuity made Mott, Mott makes industry.

MOTT: Very happy. Very happy indeed. Let's have that once more with lung. Lots of lung.

CHRISTIAN: Ingenuity made Mott, Mott makes industry.

MOTT: Not bad. It's good. Youth refreshes. Of course you don't expect to be paid much for that.

CHRISTIAN: No. But I think it's good.

MOTT: Oh, it's good. Youth refreshes. Well, you're not kidding us, son, I can see that.

HOW: He's not, Steve.

MOTT: No. At the risk of sounding too full of myself, which I do not want to sound. On the other hand I'd like to sketch in my general attitude. Towards the way I personally tackle things. Don't get the idea that I think of myself as a king or anything. But I like to acquire the evidences of man's creative impulse from outside my own orbit. But, sadly, not many are blessed with the creative impulse, but, of course, there's the repulsive creative impulse too. We won't go into that. But if there are bright brains I don't care what kind of head you got the brains in.

CHRISTIAN *putting a hand to head.*

Your head's all right, Christian, don't get nervous. But a head, square, ten feet high or like a ping-pong ball is all right so long as it works. But don't let me sound like a king. So I think you have a future, Christian. Now what about the past.

HOW: Steve, I've been through his past with him.

MOTT: Once more, fast, won't hurt.

HOW: Thought we could get around to it later. Past is fine.

MOTT: I'm interested. At that party back there, that night, Christian, you had a lot of pretty pertinent things to say with maybe a few impertinent. What have you been working at?

HOW: Steve.

MOTT: Howard, will you give the boy a chance.

HOW: Steve, do you think, with the pressure of time, that we should discuss this now?

MOTT: It has always been my habit to discuss things now. Because after now might be the hereafter, you get me? Christian's been out of college a while.

HOW: But, Christian, here is a peculiar case.

MOTT: Why?

HOW: I think his creative qualities are rare.

MOTT: That so?

HOW: Well ... (*a hand towards* CHRISTIAN) you've heard him yourself, Steve, a natural alacrity with words.

MOTT: Howard, press the button there for the curtains.

HOW *steps to wall, curtain swings open, a pair of binoculars hang.*

I don't usually show people this. But I want you to look out there, Howard. See any barges out there, going past the Statue of Liberty. Know what they are.

HOW: I think I do, Steve.

MOTT: Well, it's a private little object lesson of mine.

HOW: I understand completely, Steve.

MOTT: Here today, gone tomorrow.

HOW: I completely understand.

MOTT: So now that nobody is misunderstood let's hear about your past career. Not that I'm buying your past, just the future. Nevertheless, past gives indication of future.

CHRISTIAN: Mr. Mott, I was employed as the star receptionist for Stars of the Forest Incorporated. A funeral parlour.

MOTT (*turning from* CHRISTIAN *to* HOW): Howard.

HOW: Yes, Steve?

MOTT: Howard.

HOW: Yes, Steve?

MOTT: Howard, I'm talking to you.

HOW: I know, Steve.

MOTT: What about this?

CHRISTIAN: I was expelled from school for lying and cheating. Didn't get my degree from college. And since I've been performing a job in which I conducted the arrangements for those finding their final resting place. And nothing unseemly ever marred proceedings.

HOW: In the nature of human relations, Steve.

MOTT: I've got my own eyes and ears, Howard. There are all kinds of relations. But let me utter three things. Life is for the living. A dime is a dime. And last and the most, a dollar is a dollar. I am not being vulgar mentioning money. I change my shirt three times a day. I also yesterday was on a plane from Washington when the steward asks me was I any relation to the Motts who had a mausoleum at Throggs Neck; when I said yes he tells me his father takes care of it. This is the curiosity of life. But young Christian here tells me he's a liar and a cheat, degreeless, and can smoothly conduct people to their final resting place. Run the Mott empire like a morgue. Now just what exactly do you take me for? Why weren't the facts laid bare in the first instance.

HOW: Don't let facts fool you, Steve.

MOTT: Don't be too hasty, Howard.

HOW: I feel most recent facts take precedence over previous.

MOTT: I am of the opinion not wanting to be a king about it that past facts forecast future facts.

HOW: You're wrong.

MOTT: Come again, Howard?

HOW: You're not exactly right in judging personalities.

CHRISTIAN (*standing up slowly*): I think I'd better go.

MOTT: Stay, Christian. We'll have this out.

CHRISTIAN (*standing*): But I didn't think I'd be coming between two people. Breaking up a friendship.

*There are looks between* MOTT *and* HOW. MOTT *emits the small chuckle.* HOW *allows some of his front teeth to show.*

I know this is a business empire, but aren't you two people friends?

MOTT: You have the habit of asking a lot of direct questions

CHRISTIAN: In the fact-finding maybe I ought to find some, that's all.

MOTT: Those don't sound like the words of a liar and a cheat. I just would like to know what the score is on you, go ahead, sit down. I don't want to be rude or hurt your feelings. But you know underneath this gentle innocent exterior of yours, you seem to throw your weight about. In fact I distinctly feel I'm being pushed. That little remark about friendship and coming between two people. Yeah. And the night at my son's party. You remember my spot. And I remember overhearing a few remarks about my house as well—

*Oh, the look of innocence of* CHRISTIAN.

—don't look innocent, about the rich new vulgarity. And don't think I planned this either, getting you up here with Mr. How to give you a working over. I was impressed but don't think that you can push us all over.

CHRISTIAN: What makes you think this—

HOW: Steve, I've never met such a candid fellow as Christian.

MOTT: Oh, you think a fellow is candid because he tells you to your face that he is a liar and a cheat. And sweated away in a funeral parlour guiding people to their final resting places. And with a little background music he starts to spout beautiful utterances. Howard, don't be so naïve. Christian here could dazzle you all night with slogans each one better than the last.

HOW: Wouldn't it be sad then, Steve, to ignore this talent?

MOTT: It just so happens I know Christian's background.

HOW: Steve, please let me in on all of this.

MOTT: You're not surprised, Christian?

HOW: I thought he was an unknown quantity to you, Steve.

CHRISTIAN: Whatever you say, Mr. Mott. But I think I really ought to be going.

MOTT: Aren't you going to abuse us a little before you leave, Christian? Call us vulgar stuffed shirts?

CHRISTIAN: What makes you think you're in a position to say that, Mr. Mott? Because you think there is nothing I can do about it?

MOTT: Don't threaten me.

CHRISTIAN: I'm not threatening you.

HOW: Please, please, let me in on this.

MOTT: And I suppose you thought that if you used a frontal assault I'd be afraid to go into this little background. What happened between yourself and your wife is your own business—

CHRISTIAN: Thanks.

MOTT: But what you do where I'm personally—

HOW: Steve, isn't there a sunny side to this situation. Christian didn't tell me he was married.

MOTT: He's not.

HOW: How does a wife come into it?

MOTT: She's out of it for keeps.

HOW: You mean she threw a seven?

MOTT: That's how Christian here got into the undertaking trade.

HOW: I hope I'm not disrespectful. This is way over my head.

CHRISTIAN: Mr. Mott wants to avoid unnecessary contacts with ghouls and charlatans.

MOTT: That's enough.

CHRISTIAN: I came here genuinely looking for a job to make money.

MOTT: And thought I didn't have the guts to tell you to your face that I know the whole score on you and that I'd let you just drift into my organization and blackmail my emotional life.

CHRISTIAN: Preposterous rot.

MOTT: Don't go all British with me.

HOW: Can't we galvanize this into a new situation from which it might be possible to evolve a solution. I think, despite the terrible things that have been said here, that underneath it all we're good-hearted people. That there is still something that could be considered constructive determined from—

MOTT: Determined to be a solve-it-all, are you, How? With your hired honey.

HOW: Nobody has ever talked to me like that before, not in the three years I've been working here.

MOTT: All right, all right, Howard, this is an emotional moment.

CHRISTIAN: Meanwhile I've been insulted, but Mr. Mott, thank you for speaking the truth.

HOW: Now there's something we can start with. If the truth was spoken, well don't we feel the better for it. Maybe?

*Good old* HOW, *the looks as he looks from* CHRISTIAN *to* MOTT.

Hasn't the air been cleared? Maybe. Just a little. Isn't it just a case where personal history has intruded needlessly, personal lives dragged in, and personalities giving vent to feelings that have just become too emotional for words—

CHRISTIAN: I have never laid a hand on my wife. When she was deceased, Mr. Mott.

MOTT: Stop being candid and embarrassing.

CHRISTIAN: It's only right that you should know. My wife's death was a blow and I said a lot of peculiar things immediately following it—

HOW: I was really proud of the impression Cornelius made on me, Steve, and I know the things you've said were tempered by some fact that could just as easily be fiction.

MOTT: Why weren't the facts laid bare, that's all, Howard, naturally what can you expect if you attempt to obscure the facts—

HOW: I'm sorry, Steve.

MOTT: Maybe I was little sudden myself, sorry to drag in your personal background like that, Christian.

CHRISTIAN: Maybe I said some things I shouldn't have said.

MOTT: Well, I guess I know I did.

HOW: We all did.

CHRISTIAN: Well, I better be going. (*Rising*)

MOTT: There's a place for you here, Christian.

HOW: Construction from confusion.

MOTT: We can use you, Christian.

HOW: Steve, I'm glad you said that.

MOTT: I'm glad I was king enough to say it.

*Curtain*

# The Sandbox

*Edward Albee (1928-    )*

## Characters

| | |
|---|---|
| The Young Man | 25.  A good-looking, well-built boy in a bathing suit. |
| Mommy | 55.  A well-dressed, imposing woman. |
| Daddy | 60.  A small man; grey, thin. |
| Grandma | 86.  A tiny, wizened woman with bright eyes. |
| The Musician | No particular age, but young would be nice. |

# EDITOR'S NOTE

*The Sandbox* is a sort of poetic coda or pendant to another, much longer, play by Albee which is a biting satire on American family life called *The American Dream*. He uses the same main characters as before, all of whom are deliberately conventional American 'types', in order to weave a kind of gentle reverie or fantasy around the death of Grandma.

There is nothing realistic about it, or meant to be. The sandbox itself, as well as being ultimately Grandma's grave, represents a sort of play-pen where Mommy and Daddy can dump a tiresome old lady who, as far as they are concerned, is in her second childhood. They are both selfish, shallow, discontented people, and to them Grandma is just the petulant baby they first carry on to the stage, and the sooner they can be decently rid of their responsibility for her the happier they will be. To us, though, Grandma soon shows herself to be a spry, humorous old lady with a bit of devilment in her yet, and a lot of the play's gently ironic atmosphere comes from the fact that she is still getting a lot more fun out of life than the callous Mommy and Daddy who think it is high time she left it.

She can still, for example, cast a roguish eye at the handsome Young Man doing his exercises. But why, exactly, does Albee choose to cast this particular young man as the Angel of Death who is soon to come for her? Partly, perhaps, because death deals so sweetly and in such a kindly way with Grandma; partly because death, both to her and, in a different way, to Mommy and Daddy, is apparently so devoid of emotion or significance. For Albee is not forgetting what the Young Man stood for in his other play. There he was 'the American dream' itself —an ideal of good looks, charming manners, just the sort of upstanding, all-American boy who would be every American parent's perfect son. But Albee was at pains to show—it was the main point of his satire—that this paragon was an empty cipher. He completely lacked emotional depth. And what Albee was saying, in the character of this Young Man, about his countrymen's attitude to life, he is saying in *The Sandbox* (though much more gently) about their reaction to death. Americans, in his view, never look beyond appearances (in *The Sandbox*, significantly enough, the Young Man says he expects to get into films, although he is plainly not even a good actor; for Hollywood, 'America's dream factory' as it has been called, is where 'stars' are made on their looks alone). These characters are faced with the ultimate reality of death, but they can see nothing in it that calls for more than a display of socially correct behaviour. Mommy and Daddy think they have done their duty if they make the right arrangements, lay on some soothing music, and wait patiently. They observe the convention of looking sad for a moment, but the reality has not touched them. The Young Man, well-meaning as he is, thinks it is just a part he has been asked to play. Even Grandma is taken a little by surprise when, having done all the right things with her bucket and spade, she finds it is not a game.

It is a wry and rather moving little fantasy, executed with the lightest touch. If you find it puzzling or inconclusive on a first reading, try it again and you will begin to savour its ironic mood. Poems should never be read just once.

# THE SANDBOX

SCENE: *A bare stage, with only the following: Near the footlights, far stage-right, two simple chairs set side by side, facing the audience; near the footlights, far stage-left, a chair facing stage-right with a music stand before it; farther back, and stage-centre, slightly elevated and raked, a large child's sandbox with a toy pail and shovel; the background is the sky, which alters from brightest day to deepest night.*

*At the beginning, it is brightest day. The* YOUNG MAN *is alone on stage, to the rear of the sandbox, and to one side. He is doing callisthenics; he does callisthenics until quite at the very end of the play. These callisthenics, employing the arms only, should suggest the beating and fluttering of wings. The* YOUNG MAN *is, after all, the Angel of Death.*

MOMMY *and* DADDY *enter from stage left,* MOMMY *first.*

MOMMY (*motioning to* DADDY): Well, here we are: this is the beach.

DADDY (*whining*): I'm cold.

MOMMY (*dismissing him with a little laugh*): Don't be silly; it's as warm as toast. Look at that nice young man over there: *he* doesn't think it's cold. (*Waves to the* YOUNG MAN) Hello.

YOUNG MAN (*with an endearing smile*): Hi!

MOMMY (*looking about*): This will do perfectly ... don't you think so, Daddy? There's sand there ... and the water beyond. What do you think, Daddy?

DADDY (*vaguely*): Whatever you say, Mommy.

MOMMY (*with the same little laugh*): Well, of course ...
whatever I say. Then, it's settled, is it?

DADDY (*shrugs*): She's *your* mother, not mine.

MOMMY: I know she's my mother. What do you take me
for? (*Pause*) All right, now; let's get on with it. (*Shouts
into the wings, stage-left*) You! Out there! You can
come in now.

*The* MUSICIAN *enters, seats himself in the chair, stage-
left, places music on the music stand, is ready to play.*

(*nods approvingly*) Very nice; very nice. Are you ready,
Daddy? Let's go get Grandma.

DADDY: Whatever you say, Mommy.

MOMMY (*leading the way out, stage-left*): Of course, whatever I say. (*To the* MUSICIAN) You can begin now.

*The* MUSICIAN *begins playing;* MOMMY *and* DADDY *exit;
the* MUSICIAN, *all the while playing, nods to the* YOUNG
MAN.

YOUNG MAN (*with the same endearing smile*): Hi!

*After a moment,* MOMMY *and* DADDY *re-enter, carrying*
GRANDMA. *She is borne in by their hands under her arm-
pits; she is quite rigid; her legs are drawn up; her feet
do not touch the ground; the expression on her ancient
face is that of puzzlement and fear.*

DADDY: Where do we put her?

MOMMY (*the same little laugh*): Wherever I say, of course.
Let me see ... well ... all right, over there ... in the
sandbox. (*Pause*) Well, what are you waiting for, Daddy?
... The sandbox!

*Together they carry* GRANDMA *over to the sandbox and
more or less dump her in.*

GRANDMA (*righting herself to a sitting position; her voice
a cross between a baby's laugh and cry*): Ahhhhhh!
Graaaaaa!

DADDY (*dusting himself*): What do we do now?

MOMMY (*to the* MUSICIAN): You can stop now.

*The* MUSICIAN *stops.*

(*To Daddy*) What do you mean, what do we do now? We go over there and sit down, of course. (*To the* YOUNG MAN) Hello there.

YOUNG MAN (*again smiling*): Hi!

MOMMY *and* DADDY *move to the chairs, stage-right, and sit down. Pause.*

GRANDMA (*same as before*): Ahhhhhh! Graaaaaa!

DADDY: Do you think ... do you think she's ... comfortable?

MOMMY (*impatiently*): How would I know?

*Pause.*

DADDY: What do we do now?

MOMMY (*as if remembering*): We ... wait. We ... sit here ... and we wait ... that's what we do.

DADDY (*after a pause*): Shall we talk to each other.

MOMMY (*with that little laugh; picking something off her dress*): Well, *you* can talk, if you want to ... if you can think of anything to *say* ... if you can think of anything *new*.

DADDY (*thinks*): No ... I suppose not.

MOMMY (*with a triumphant laugh*): Of course not!

GRANDMA (*banging the toy shovel against the pail*): Haaaaaa! Ah-haaaaaa!

MOMMY (*out over the audience*): Be quiet, Grandma ... just be quiet, and wait.

GRANDMA *throws a shovelful of sand at* MOMMY.

(*Still out over the audience*) She's throwing sand at me! You stop that, Grandma; you stop throwing sand at Mommy! (*To Daddy*) She's throwing sand at me.

DADDY *looks around at* GRANDMA, *who screams at him.*

GRANDMA: GRAAAAAA!

MOMMY: Don't look at her. Just ... sit here ... be very still ... and wait. (*To the* MUSICIAN) You ... uh ... you go ahead and do whatever it is you do.

*The* MUSICIAN *plays.*

MOMMY *and* DADDY *are fixed, staring out beyond the audience.* GRANDMA *looks at them, looks at the* MUSICIAN, *looks at the sandbox, throws down the shovel.*

GRANDMA: Ah-haaaaaa! Graaaaaa! (*Looks for reaction; gets none. Now ... directly to the audience*) Honestly! What a way to treat an old woman! Drag her out of the house ... stick her in a car ... bring her out here from the city ... dump her in a pile of sand ... and leave her here to set. I'm eighty-six years old! I was married when I was seventeen. To a farmer. He died when I was thirty. (*To the* MUSICIAN) Will you stop that, please?

MUSICIAN *stops playing.*

I'm a feeble old woman ... how do you expect anybody to hear me over that peep! peep! peep! (*To herself*) There's no respect around here. (*To the* YOUNG MAN) There's no respect around here!

YOUNG MAN (*same smile*): Hi!

GRANDMA (*after a pause, a mild double-take, continues, to the audience*): My husband died when I was thirty— (*indicates* MOMMY)—and I had to raise that big cow over there all by my lonesome. You can imagine what *that* was like. Lordy! (*To the* YOUNG MAN) Where'd they get *you*?

YOUNG MAN: Oh ... I've been around for a while.

GRANDMA: I'll bet you have! Heh, heh, heh, Will you look at you!

YOUNG MAN (*flexing his muscles*): Isn't that something? (*Continues his callisthenics*)

GRANDMA: Boy, oh boy; I'll say. Pretty good.

YOUNG MAN (*sweetly*): I'll say.

GRANDMA: Where ya from?

YOUNG MAN: Southern California.

GRANDMA (*nodding*): Figgers; figgers. What's your name, honey?

YOUNG MAN: I don't know ...

GRANDMA (*to the audience*): Bright, too!

YOUNG MAN: I mean ... I mean, they haven't given me one yet ... the studio ...

GRANDMA (*giving him the once-over*): You don't say ... you don't say. Well ... uh, I've got to talk some more ... don't you go 'way.

YOUNG MAN: Oh, no.

GRANDMA (*turning her attention back to the audience*): Fine; fine. (*Then, once more, back to the* YOUNG MAN) You're ... you're an actor, hunh?

YOUNG MAN (*beaming*): Yes. I am.

GRANDMA (*to the audience again; shrugs*): I'm smart that way. *Anyhow,* I had to raise ... *that* over there all by my lonesome; and what's next to her there ... that's what she married. Rich? I tell you ... money, money, money. They took me off the *farm* ... which was real decent of them ... and they moved me into the big town house with *them* ... fixed a nice place for me under the stove ... gave me an army blanket ... and my own dish ... my very own dish! So, what have I got to complain about? Nothing, of course. I'm not complaining. (*She looks up at the sky, shouts to someone off stage*) Shouldn't it be getting dark now, dear?

*The lights dim; night comes on. The* MUSICIAN *begins*

*to play; it becomes deepest night. There are spots on all
the players, including the* YOUNG MAN, *who is, of course,
continuing his callisthenics.*

DADDY (*stirring*): It's night-time.

MOMMY: Shhhh. Be still ... wait.

DADDY (*whining*): It's so hot.

MOMMY: Shhhh. Be still ... wait.

GRANDMA (*to herself*): That's better. Night. (*To the*
MUSICIAN) Honey, do you play all through this part?

*The* MUSICIAN *nods.*

Well, keep it nice and soft; that's a good boy.

*The* MUSICIAN *nods again; plays softly.*

That's nice.

*There's an off-stage rumble.*

DADDY (*starting*): What was that?

MOMMY (*beginning to weep*): It was nothing.

DADDY: It was ... it was ... thunder ... or a wave breaking ... or something.

MOMMY (*whispering, through her tears*): It was an off-
stage rumble ... and you know what *that* means ...

DADDY: I forget ...

MOMMY (*barely able to talk*): It means the time has come
for poor Grandma ... and I can't bear it!

DADDY (*vacantly*): I ... I suppose you've got to be brave.

GRANDMA (*mocking*): That's right, kid; be brave. You'll
bear up; you'll get over it.

*Another off-stage rumble ... louder.*

MOMMY: Ohhhhhhhhhh ... poor Grandma ... poor
Grandma.

GRANDMA (*to* MOMMY): I'm fine! I'm all right! It hasn't
happened yet!

*A violent off-stage rumble. All the lights go out, save the spot on the* YOUNG MAN; *the* MUSICIAN *stops playing.*

MOMMY: Ohhhhhhhhh ... Ohhhhhhhhh ...

*Silence.*

GRANDMA: Don't put the lights up yet ... I'm not ready; I'm not quite ready.

*Silence.*

All right, dear ... I'm about done.
*The lights come up again, to brightest day; the* MUSICIAN *begins to play.* GRANDMA *is discovered, still in the sandbox, lying on her side, propped up on an elbow, halfcovered, busily shovelling sand over herself.*

GRANDMA (*muttering*): I don't know how I'm supposed to do anything with this goddam toy shovel ...

DADDY: Mommy! It's daylight!

MOMMY (*brightly*): So it is! Well! Our long night is over. We must put away our tears, take off our mourning ... and face the future. It's our duty.

GRANDMA (*still shovelling; mimicking*): ... take off our mourning ... face the future ... Lordy!

MOMMY *and* DADDY *rise, stretch.* MOMMY *waves to the* YOUNG MAN.

YOUNG MAN (*with that smile*): Hi!

GRANDMA *plays dead.* MOMMY *and* DADDY *go over to look at her; she is a little more than half buried in the sand; the toy shovel is in her hands, which are crossed on her breast.*

MOMMY (*before the sandbox; shaking her head*): Lovely! It's ... it's hard to be sad ... she looks ... so happy. (*With pride and conviction*) It pays to do things well. (*To the* MUSICIAN) All right, you can stop now, if you want to. I mean, stay around for a swim, or something:

it's all right with us. (*She sighs heavily*) Well, **Daddy**
... off we go.

DADDY: Brave Mommy!

MOMMY: Brave Daddy!

*They exit, stage-left.*

GRANDMA (*after they leave; lying quite still*): It pays to do
thing well ... Boy, oh boy! (*She tries to sit up*) ... well,
kids ... (*but she finds she can't*) I ... I can't get up. I
... I can't move ...

*The* YOUNG MAN *stops his callisthenics, nods to the*
MUSICIAN, *walks over to* GRANDMA, *kneels down by the*
*sandbox.*

I ... can't move ...

YOUNG MAN: Shhhh ... be very still ...

GRANDMA: I ... I can't move.

YOUNG MAN: Uh ... ma'am; I ... I have a line here.

GRANDMA: Oh, I'm sorry, sweetie; you go right ahead.

YOUNG MAN: I am ... uh ...

GRANDMA: Take your time, dear.

YOUNG MAN (*prepares; delivers the line like a real amateur*):
I am the Angel of Death. I am ... uh ... I am come for
you.

GRANDMA: What ... wha ... (*then, with resignation*)
ohhh ... ohhh, I see.

*The* YOUNG MAN *bends over, kisses* GRANDMA *gently on*
*the forehead.*

GRANDMA (*her eyes closed, her hands folded on her breast*
*again, the shovel between her hands, a sweet smile on*
*her face*): Well ... that was very nice, dear ...

YOUNG MAN (*still kneeling*): Shhhhh ... be still ...

GRANDMA: What I meant was ... you did that very well,
dear ...

TT—G

YOUNG MAN (*blushing*): ... oh ...

GRANDMA: No; I mean it. You've got that ... you've got a quality.

YOUNG MAN (*with his endearing smile*): Oh ... thank you; thank you very much ... ma'am.

GRANDMA (*slowly; softly—as the* YOUNG MAN *puts his hands on top of hers*): You're ... you're welcome ... dear.

*Tableau. The* MUSICIAN *continues to play as the curtain slowly comes down.*

# Then . . .

*David Campton (1924-     )*

## Characters

Mr. Phythick
Miss Europe

# EDITOR'S NOTE

Mankind's ability to wipe itself off the earth has become the central issue of our time. A shadow of disaster hangs over every one of us, but do we—can we—individually do anything about it? David Campton is a young writer whose plays often deal, in a serio-comic spirit, with this theme, particularly with the way we too often let other people get away with murder (literally, in one of his sketches) by not bothering to know or care about what goes on outside our private, day-to-day concerns. His two characters in this play, Beauty and Brains (helpless beauty and useless brains) are people who did not know or care to know, and now they find themselves sole survivors of the final catastrophe. Were they in any way to blame for what happened? It is hinted that it was an ex-student of Phythick's who actually caused the atomization of the human race. 'I am not responsible for my pupils, though', Phythick hastily explains. Well, that, of course, is the big question. Which of us is not responsible?

But there is an ironic twist in this play. It has been more by good luck than good management that these two apparent innocents have survived, and the paper bags over their heads could be, if you like, a symbol of their respective types of blindness—of what makes *him* afraid of responsibility, and what makes *her* utterly dependent on other people's decisions. Yet these same paper bags are what saved their lives. Coming together in their pathetic-comic quandary, they appear to have learned a little bit of courage and a little bit of wisdom, just enough, possibly, to start afresh. But is it too late? Can they now take off their paper bags? And that question the author leaves tantalizingly open, because he is, after all, really talking about us.

*Then* ... is an excellent example of a recent type of play which has been called Comedy of Menace (the term seems actually to have been coined around 1961 to describe the early plays of Harold Pinter like *The Birthday Party* and *The Dumb Waiter*). They are plays which try to capture the sort of undefined fear which haunts our post-war world and which was vividly anticipated in the novels of Franz Kafka. But if they are mirrors of our anxiety, they are comic mirrors, provoking nervous laughter. *Then* ... is a chilling little play, but at the same time a funny and rather touching one. It is also a good example of absolute simplicity in staging. It could be acted in any darkened room with a single light. The paper bags, by the way, can have eye-holes cut in them.

# THEN ...

*Darkness. A* MAN *speaks.*

PHYTHICK: It's not much to ask. I've never asked for a lot. I shouldn't have got it anyway. Whatever I wanted. ... A little light. Just a glimmer. Just enough to see to die by ...

*The moon comes out.* PHYTHICK *is a wisp of a man in an old mackintosh several sizes too large for him. Over his head he wears a brown paper bag. He is sitting on a short flight of steps.*

Oh, that's too sudden. I don't want to die suddenly. Not like all the others, whispered out in a puff. But I don't want to die slowly either. A man ought to have the right to die the way he wants. It should be easy. A piece of string, an old razor blade, an overdose of aspirin ... But what's the use? Why take all the responsibility when a falling brick might do as well? Why die at all? Why live at all? Why sit here asking questions? ... I'm hungry ... Oh, it's not fair. The fools in authority make mistakes, and who has to suffer? Who? There should be no fools in authority. There should be no authority. A man should be left to himself ... I don't want to be left to myself. Dust. All that's left. Dust. All my hopes. All my chances. Dust. Dust. Dust. Dust. ...

*A* GIRL *walks by. She is smartly dressed with a good figure. In one hand she carries an umbrella, and in the other a vanity box. Over her head she wears a brown paper bag.*

PHYTHICK *watches her absently. When she is almost out of sight he wakes up suddenly.*

Oh, I say. You there. Please. (*Whistles*)

*The* GIRL *stops and turns. Then comes back.*

GIRL: You called?

PHYTHICK: Yes.

GIRL: Why?

PHYTHICK: You're a girl.

GIRL: You call after girls?

PHYTHICK: Certainly not. I thought . . .

GIRL: I'd missed you.

PHYTHICK: That's right.

GIRL: I thought you were . . .

PHYTHICK: I'm alive.

GIRL: So am I.

PHYTHICK: Where are you going?

GIRL: Nowhere. Just going.

PHYTHICK: Would you like to stay? Here. For a while?

GIRL: If you like.

PHYTHICK: I don't usually call after—people in the streets.

GIRL: In my profession I have to be careful who I talk to. Quite famous people write for appointments . . .

PHYTHICK: The last time I approached anyone in the street was to ask for small change—for a telephone call . . .

GIRL: The press were never granted an interview in less than a week, but I think that was because I had a contract. I—I'm glad you called.

PHYTHICK: I—I'm glad you came back.

GIRL: My manager would be cross if he knew. There was something in my contract about talking to strange men. I'm sorry, because I'm interested in men. They're not like girls.

PHYTHICK: I have—noticed a—difference.

GIRL (*casually*): Is this Hyde Park Corner?

PHYTHICK: Piccadilly Circus.

GIRL: It's changed.

PHYTHICK: Eros disappeared. I don't know why. There must be some plausible theory.

GIRL: He—didn't have a paper bag round his head.

PHYTHICK: I shouldn't have imagined he needed one.

GIRL: They saved us—didn't they?

PHYTHICK: The ...

GIRL: Yes.

PHYTHICK: They must have done. I couldn't follow the theory myself, but I trusted it. Fortunately my faith was justified. When the only other person I see who has escaped the—disaster wears a brown paper bag ...

GIRL: Oh? Who?

PHYTHICK: Who?

GIRL: Who was the only other person you see—saw?

PHYTHICK: Why, you, of course.

GIRL: Oh, yes. I'm alive, too, aren't I? I—hadn't thought about that. When you're alive you don't seem to notice it. Do you? Being alive, I mean. And when you're dead you don't have to bother.

PHYTHICK: Perhaps I ought to introduce myself.

GIRL: Please do.

PHYTHICK: My name is Phythick. I am—a schoolmaster.

GIRL: Oh, yes?

PHYTHICK: I teach physics and higher mathematics. I—taught—physics and higher mathematics. I am quite attached to mathematics. They dispense with words, you see. They are like unemotional music. Sine over cosine equals tangent. No confusion there. I was a comparatively successful teacher. A few of my pupils became chiefs of nuclear research. One was actually knighted. Another was responsible for important developments in hetrodynamic deterrents. He—he always thought it possible to reduce living organisms to dust

—by remote control. I am not responsible for my pupils though. I merely pass on knowledge, you understand. It is up to them what they do with it. Most of them became butchers, brokers, or insurance agents. I am not responsible if they advance their careers in hetrodynamic deterrents.

GIRL: Of course not.

PHYTHICK: Do you think so? Do you really think so?

GIRL: Of course. You just told me so.

PHYTHICK: Do you always believe everything you're told?

GIRL: Don't you?

PHYTHICK: I—try to strike a balance ... Who are you? What is your name?

GIRL: You don't know? It doesn't show?

PHYTHICK: A great deal shows, but not your name.

GIRL: I'm Miss Europe.

PHYTHICK: Miss Europe?

GIRL: This year's Miss Europe. I'd have been Miss World next year. Everybody said I was the only girl with the correct poise and the perfect measurements.

PHYTHICK: Perfect indeed, Miss Europe.

GIRL: I was only fifteen when I started. I was Miss Chocolate Box and Miss Holiday Camp that year. My measurements weren't so perfect then—too much here, and not enough there: but I worked and worked. Diets and exercises and interviews and agents. I worked my way up to the top. I'd have been Miss World next year— only now there doesn't seem to be a world to be a Miss of. Oh, I worked. I learned. Oh, my goodness, yes. I learned how to walk. I knew which of the judges to smile at, and which to wiggle at. They used my hair to advertise shampoo, and my smile for razor blades. I signed contracts. I wasn't to get married or fall in love.

I wasn't to be seen with anybody but the right people.
And this year I was Miss Europe.

PHYTHICK: My congratulations. I believe the judges were
right.

GIRL: Why, thank you. It wasn't much use, though, was
it? I mean—there'll never be any more competitions.
There's nobody left to have competitions with. Just dust.
Just piles of dust. Black dust and white dust and red
dust and yellow dust.

PHYTHICK: Please. Please. One doesn't mention such things.

GIRL: Are you afraid?

PHYTHICK: Aren't you?

GIRL: I don't know. I never thought about it. I was never
any good at thinking. Now you'll think I'm stupid.

PHYTHICK: How can you see as much as a speck of dust
and not wonder ...

GIRL: I wondered all right. There was so much. Especially
in the room where I left my manager. I tried to use the
vacuum cleaner. Do you think they switched the electricity off?

PHYTHICK: The power station is unmanned.

GIRL: And that cuts off the electricity? Then that was
why I couldn't get anything on the telly either.

PHYTHICK: The television?

GIRL: They tell you what to do, you know. They showed
me how to use my brown paper bag. They said it was
the surest way not to be atomised. And they were right.
I always believed what they told me. I'm not taking
this bag off until they tell me either.

PHYTHICK: No one will ever tell you anything on television again.

GIRL: Then it stays on. I'm taking no chances.

PHYTHICK: Does this—accident mean no more to you than
no electricity and no television?

GIRL: I noticed them first. Perhaps I shall notice other things later.

PHYTHICK: Don't you wonder which fool allowed this to happen? Didn't you ask yourself who was to blame?

GIRL: I didn't know anyone allowed it. I thought it just happened—like a wet Bank Holiday.

PHYTHICK: Oh no. Oh no, no, no, no, no, no. Whitehall blundered. They gave the fanatics in hetrodynamic deterrents carte blanche. Can you imagine that? They deputed absolute authority for the world to be destroyed.

GIRL: Was it destroyed?

PHYTHICK: It has been granulated.

GIRL: You're clever to think of that. I admire clever men.

PHYTHICK: I have always prided myself upon clear thinking. I am not a proud man, but I flatter myself that I have a mind.

GIRL: Oh, you have. You have just that.

PHYTHICK: I have reasoned exactly how this—disaster occurred, and who is responsible for it. I always think better when I'm hungry.

GIRL: Are you hungry now?

PHYTHICK: Starving.

GIRL: Isn't that lucky? I packed a lunch in my vanity box. (*She looks inside her vanity box.*)

PHYTHICK *faints.*

I've some sausage rolls and some cornish pasties. They're terrible for the figure, but you're not worried about that, are you? That's right. Lie back and make yourself comfortable. There are things at the bottom that might be potato crisps ... Why, Mr. Thing. Mr. Thing ... Aren't you listening? Are you ill? Can't you hear me? It's me. Me. Oh! Please don't die. I've just laid out the supper. Mr. Thing. Mr. Thing. Won't you have a sausage roll?

PHYTHICK *stirs.*

Oh, thank goodness you're waking up. Do you feel better now? I brought some cold milk in a thermos flask.

PHYTHICK (*feebly*): Thank you. Thank you so much. I believe it was the first shock. The first shock of the promised land is always overwhelming.

GIRL: Your milk.

PHYTHICK: Thank you. Is it safe?

GIRL: It's Jersey milk.

PHYTHICK: There was food in the shops, but I hesitated.

GIRL: I kept all this in a biscuit tin. Food in tins is safe. They said so.

PHYTHICK: Oh, the luxury of being able to eat again without risk.

GIRL: My uncle once choked on a sardine tail.

PHYTHICK: I don't object to risks, mind you.

GIRL: We can eat sardines because I brought a fish knife.

PHYTHICK: Personal risks. But no one has the right to take risks which affect other persons. That is called responsibility.

GIRL: I haven't eaten for so long. I walked and slept and seemed to forget about eating. All the clocks seemed to have stopped. I just didn't know whether it was eating time or not. And there was no one I could ask.

PHYTHICK (*with a chuckle like the rustle of dry paper*): Oh, Miss Europe, did anyone ever tell you that you are utterly enchanting?

GIRL: Are you fond of potato crisps? They called me the teenagers' sweetheart. They called me that on television so it must have been true.

PHYTHICK: Why didn't I meet you years ago?

GIRL: I was a career girl then. I ought to have brought the bottled plums. We would never have met because I had a bodyguard. Just like a real Princess. That was a long ago as Miss Rubber Tyre, when I was the Pork Sausage Queen.

PHYTHICK: I locked my study door, and devoted myself to figures. It was wrong of me.

GIRL: I had a boy friend when I was fifteen. Oh, I forgot the salt, too. He's married now with four babies. He wanted me to run away to Gretna Green with him, and have babies. They taste much better with salt. It's too late now. I can't have babies because of my contract.

PHYTHICK: I'm quite light headed. It must have been my prolonged fast. It could hardly have been the milk.

GIRL: Won't you eat your cornish pasty? I don't know what to do. Really I don't. I just get up and walk about, and sit down again. When I was little, my dad used to tell me what to do, and then my agent and manager told me what to do. But they're all gone now. Crumbled away.

PHYTHICK (*about to take a bite of pasty*): Dusty. (*He blows it, and is about to take another bite when the significance of this strikes him*).

GIRL: Have some more milk to help it down.

PHYTHICK: Thank you, Miss Europe ...

GIRL: Do you like my gloves?

PHYTHICK: Oh. Oh dear, oh dear, oh dear.

GIRL: Something wrong?

PHYTHICK: Everything. We should never have begun like this. I called after you in the street. I whistled. I behaved like a hooligan. Anything I say to you now will be coloured and distorted. You will say only a hooligan could make advances like that.

GIRL: Oh, I'd never say that. I've seen them. Oh, my

goodness, yes. The front row faces in the beauty contests. Eyes running like hot fingers over my swim suit, and wicked little minds that stayed with me from there until bed-time. You're not like them. You're out of the top drawer.

PHYTHICK: Do you really believe that?

GIRL: Don't you want me to?

PHYTHICK: Of course.

GIRL: Then tell me to.

PHYTHICK: You must believe me.

GIRL: Very well, then. I shall.

PHYTHICK: Miss Europe ... I want you to understand that this is no hurried statement. Although it may appear to be composed on the spur of the moment, it has a lifetime's reasoning behind it.

GIRL: I know perfectly well what you are going to say, and I might as well tell you here and now that I agree with every word of it.

PHYTHICK: The very act of living involves us in responsibility. We cannot cross a street without affecting the lives of others. There is more responsibility than a single person can bear.

GIRL: Oh, Mr. Thing ...

PHYTHICK: I warm towards you. Do you know that? I ...

GIRL: I feel something about you too. I ...

PHYTHICK: I feel your proximity glowing in me like old wine. I ...

GIRL: I felt it the very second I heard you call me. I ...

PHYTHICK: I want to stretch out my hands to touch you, I ...

GIRL: I just had to turn back to you. I ...

PHYTHICK: I want to hold you in my arms and crush you to me.

GIRL: I think we ought to sit closer.

PHYTHICK: You think so too? Oh, Miss Europe ... Do you really believe that such things can happen?

GIRL: Something inside—told me.

*He clasps her in his arms. Their heads come together, but do not touch. They freeze in this position for a few seconds. Then they straighten. There is a pause. In fact there is a long pause between each of the next few speeches. He laughs. A short, dry, nervous laugh.*

PHYTHICK: Ridiculous.

GIRL: Silly.

PHYTHICK: For one minute ...

GIRL: I thought so too.

PHYTHICK: That I was making love to a brown paper bag.

GIRL: It's a good bag.

PHYTHICK: I've never seen a better bag.

GIRL: I bought it specially. I chose it carefully.

PHYTHICK: I should have expected that.

GIRL: I tried on every bag in the shop. It was expensive. I couldn't have an ordinary bag.

PHYTHICK: I didn't have time to choose.

GIRL: It was sudden, wasn't it?

PHYTHICK: I was in the tuck-shop at the time. I grabbed the first bag that came to my hand. And the only protective clothing I could find belonged to the matron.

GIRL: It—suits you.

PHYTHICK: It doesn't fit.

GIRL: Before you remembered—my brown paper bag— what were you going to do?

PHYTHICK: Kiss you.

GIRL: Are you crying?

PHYTHICK: A little.

GIRL: Because you didn't kiss me?

PHYTHICK: My bag had onions in.

GIRL: Did you know that I'd fallen in love with you?

PHYTHICK: I wanted you to.

GIRL: What can we do now?

PHYTHICK: Take them off?

GIRL: Is it safe?

PHYTHICK: I don't know. I don't know.

GIRL: They were going to tell us on television when it was safe ... I'd take it off if you told me.

PHYTHICK: My dear, that's very touching ...

GIRL: Then you'll tell me to?

PHYTHICK: No! I couldn't accept the responsibility. It might not be safe. How should I feel if you crumbled to dust before my eyes? I'd be hurt.

GIRL: You could risk it.

PHYTHICK: I could not. I—I'm too fond of you to allow you to take risks.

GIRL: Then I must keep it on?

PHYTHICK: You must decide that for yourself.

GIRL: But I can't. I can't.

PHYTHICK: I'm only afraid for you, my dear. I couldn't have you on my conscience.

GIRL: Hold my hand.

PHYTHICK: There's nothing to come between us really. No mountains, gorges, cataracts, no seas or stormy floods, no friends, relations, rivals, or previous attachments. If we truly want each other, we are free to follow our fancies.

GIRL: You talk so beautifully.

PHYTHICK: Do I? I never thought that I could talk. My tongue must have run away with me.

GIRL: Let it run away again.

PHYTHICK: You remind me of old, forgotten, far-off things. 'Behold thou art fair, my love. Behold thou art fair.'

GIRL: I'm a brunette.

PHYTHICK: I want to run my fingers through your curls—
your hair does curl? And see my soul reflected in the
deep, blue pools of your eyes ...

GIRL: Brown.

PHYTHICK: In the deep brown pools of your eyes.

GIRL: That's like poetry.

PHYTHICK: I have feelings surging in me that hardly
become a mathematics master. I want to crush my lips
against your rosebud mouth ... Is it a rosebud mouth?

GIRL: It's not very large.

PHYTHICK: You—must have a pretty face.

GIRL: I thought so once.

PHYTHICK: You do—have a face?

GIRL: You tell me.

PHYTHICK: How can I? I've never seen it.

GIRL: How do I know I've got a face at all if you won't
tell me?

PHYTHICK: How do I know what face you've got when it's
hidden under a bag?

GIRL: Shall I take it off?

PHYTHICK: No. Why are you trying to push responsibility
on to me?

GIRL (*accusingly*): You're afraid. (*She gets up and walks
despondently away*) I'm no use to you at all. I'm so
dependent and you're such—so—such ...

PHYTHICK: Coward. That's your word, isn't it? (*He gets up*).
Wave length times frequency equals the speed of sound
... I was a fool to think a female more trustworthy than
a formula.

GIRL: I trust you.

PHYTHICK: I'll walk this way, and ...

GIRL: We know, don't we?

PHYTHICK: About?

GIRL: Each other.

PHYTHICK: Too much.

GIRL: How far?

PHYTHICK: To the sea . . .

GIRL: And then?

PHYTHICK: Who knows?

GIRL: I can't blow my nose.

PHYTHICK: It's for the best.

GIRL: I believe you.

PHYTHICK: Don't.

GIRL: You're—not walking.

PHYTHICK: I sat too long.

GIRL: Oh, well. I'll find someone else soon enough. Why, I thought I was the only person left in the whole wide world, and then there you were—sitting in the middle of Piccadilly Circus.

PHYTHICK: Goodbye.

GIRL: And you needn't think I hadn't looked for someone else because I had. I rang up all my friends, but they were all out.

PHYTHICK: I said—goodbye.

GIRL: You ate my supper.

PHYTHICK: We are the only ones. We are the only ones in the world. We are the world.

GIRL: Goodbye.

PHYTHICK: Goodbye.

GIRL: Oh, Mr. Thing . . .

PHYTHICK: Miss Europe . . .

*They turn and run into each other's arms.*

There. There.

GIRL: I want a man to put his arms around me.

PHYTHICK: Here they are.

GIRL: I want to feel safe and comfortable.

PHYTHICK: You are. You are.

GIRL: I don't care tuppence about any silly old paper bags. And I'm happy as long as I can hear your voice. Talk to me. Talk to me.

PHYTHICK: I have a theory.

GIRL: It's wonderful to hear you talk.

PHYTHICK: Why we are the only two to be wearing paper bags.

GIRL: Your voice is so comfortable—like a deep, warm blanket.

PHYTHICK: You put yours on because you always do as you are told. I put mine on because I was—nervous.

GIRL: Sweet, soft, loving words. I adore every one of them.

PHYTHICK: But no one else bothered. Why?

GIRL: I don't ask questions any more. I just listen.

PHYTHICK: Everyone had heard the propaganda so much that they were used to it. They weren't afraid of the hetrodynamic deterrents any more. It was as familiar as Father Christmas. It was cosy. It appeared on every television screen in every home. It was a household pet.

GIRL: It was a clean bomb.

PHYTHICK: Exactly.

GIRL: I loved it. It sounded so hygienic. Everyone said that it was a good thing. And it was on our side. Go on talking.

PHYTHICK: What more is there to say?

GIRL: Nothing. Just cuddle close to me.

*They do that. Their heads touch. The brown paper crinkles. They sit sharply upright.*

We crinkled.

PHYTHICK: We were bound to. Paper does crinkle.

GIRL: Paper tears.

*Pause.*

PHYTHICK: It's dangerous.

GIRL: We mustn't sit closely, or kiss, or anything.

PHYTHICK: We might tear.

GIRL (*tearfully*): It's difficult—being in love. Isn't it.

PHYTHICK: We do love each other, don't we?

GIRL: We need each other.

PHYTHICK (*hopelessly*): We can always hold hands.

*Pause.*

GIRL: We shall never really come together, shall we? We shall never know each other as two people ought to know each other?

PHYTHICK: Never.

GIRL: Never?

PHYTHICK: Never.

GIRL: Not as long as we wear these paper-bags.

PHYTHICK: Not until I'm unafraid.

GIRL: Not until I understand.

*Pause.*

GIRL: We shall always wear these paper-bags ... Shan't we?

PHYTHICK: Of course. Unless ...

GIRL: Yes?

*Pause.*

PHYTHICK (*an idea stirring*): We ...

GIRL (*hope dawning*): Go on ...

PHYTHICK: Then ...

*He raises his hands to his paper bag. A cloud comes over the moon.*

# The Black and White

# Last to go

## Two short sketches

*Harold Pinter (1930-    )*

## Characters

# EDITOR'S NOTE

From being an unknown actor and spare-time poet barely five years ago, Harold Pinter has become one of England's most interesting and certainly most influential younger dramatists, and his reputation has been won, above all, by the quality of his dialogue, which can be seen at its most typical in these two sketches—'complete plays which just happen to be four minutes long', as he calls them. The main characteristic of this dialogue is an uncanny realism. Once your ears have been alerted by Pinter, you keep overhearing snatches of conversation in real life which sound exactly as he might have written them, pauses, repetitions, absurd *non-sequiturs* and all.

Pinter, however, is no mere tape-recorder of conversation but a most precise artist, and it is sometimes said against him that his way of writing can sound like a mannerism. 'Pinteresque' dialogue, in fact, has often been imitated and is not difficult to parody. But two things make genuine Pinter dialogue superior to any caricature of it. One is the subtlety of its rhythms. When the pauses and repetitions are observed with the accuracy on which the author insists, their effect (paradoxically enough for 'realistic' dialogue) is almost that of free verse, and an illuminating comparison can be made with the free-verse rhythms in parts of T. S. Eliot's *The Waste Land* and *Sweeney Agonistes*. Pinter also manages to suggest that, although what is spoken aloud may in itself sound trivial, something a great deal more significant lies behind the words. And that unspoken something is the real personality of the speaker, that hidden part of him which, like the submerged nine-tenths of an iceberg, can only be guessed at, never known for certain.

It can never be known, Pinter argues, because people are unable, or perhaps even unwilling, to reveal themselves fully in speech. Yet they need to talk to one another, need to establish frail bridgeheads of communication if only to keep human contact alive and ward off loneliness (both these dialogues, one notices, take place in the lonely hours of late evening, between people who seem to have nowhere special to go, nothing special to do). Yet they can never really tell their inmost thoughts to each other. Words are too difficult. And compromising. So they fall into these indeterminate makeshifts of conversation. Here is what Pinter himself has said about it: 'I feel that instead of any ability to communicate, there is a deliberate evasion of communication. Communication itself between people [by which Pinter means any attempt to reveal one's inner self or to probe into the soul of another] is so frightening that rather than do that there is continual cross-talk, continual talking about other things rather that what is at the root of their relationship.'

This 'evasion' and 'cross-talk', clearly felt in these two hauntingly vivid little glimpses of unnoticed lives, can sound funny as well as true. Nothing, in either piece, 'happens', except that two old tramp-women, and two men at a coffee-stall, come briefly alive, 'worthy of our interest' as Pinter says, 'primarily because they *are*, they exist, not because of any moral the author may draw from them'. In the first sketch, *The Black and White* is the name of an all-night milk-bar which until recently actually existed in Fleet Street. The second, of course, was written when there were still three evening papers in London and not two, as now.

# THE BLACK AND WHITE

*The* FIRST OLD WOMAN *is sitting at a milk bar table. Small. A* SECOND OLD WOMAN *approaches. Tall. She is carrying two bowls of soup, which are covered by two plates, on each of which is a slice of bread. She puts the bowls down on the table carefully.*

SECOND: You see that one come up and speak to me at the counter? (*She takes the bread plates off the bowls, takes two spoons from her pocket, and places the bowls, plates and spoons.*)

FIRST: You got the bread, then?

SECOND: I didn't know how I was going to carry it. In the end I put the plates on top of the soup.

FIRST: I like a bit of bread with my soup.

*They begin the soup. Pause.*

SECOND: Did you see that one come up and speak to me at the counter?

FIRST: Who?

SECOND: Comes up to me, he says, hullo, he says, what's the time by your clock? Bloody liberty. I was just standing there getting your soup.

FIRST: It's tomato soup.

SECOND: What's the time by your clock? he says.

FIRST: I bet you answered him back.

SECOND: I told him all right. Go on, I said, why don't you get back into your scraghole, I said, clear off out of it before I call a copper.

*Pause.*

FIRST: I not long got here.

SECOND: Did you get the all-night bus?

FIRST: I got the all-night bus straight here.

SECOND: Where from?

FIRST: Marble Arch.

SECOND: Which one?

FIRST: The two-nine-four, that takes me all the way to Fleet Street.

SECOND: So does the two-nine-one. (*pause*) I see you talking to two strangers as I come in. You want to stop talking to strangers, old piece of boot like you, you mind who you talk to.

FIRST: I wasn't talking to any strangers.

*Pause. The* FIRST OLD WOMAN *follows the progress of a bus through the window.*

That's another all-night bus gone down. (*pause*) That was a two-nine-seven. (*pause*) I've never been up that way. (*pause*) I've been down to Liverpool Street.

SECOND: That's up the other way.

FIRST: I don't fancy going down there, down Fulham way, and all up there.

SECOND: Uh-uh.

FIRST: I've never fancied that direction much.

*Pause.*

SECOND: How's your bread?

*Pause.*

FIRST: Eh?

SECOND: Your bread.

FIRST: All right. How's yours?

*Pause.*

SECOND: They don't charge for the bread if you have soup.

FIRST: They do if you have tea.

SECOND: If you have tea they do. (*pause*) You talk to strangers they'll take you in. Mind my word. Coppers'll take you in.

FIRST: I don't talk to strangers.

SECOND: They took me away in the wagon once.

FIRST: They didn't keep you though.

SECOND: They didn't keep me, but that was only because they took a fancy to me. They took a fancy to me when they got me in the wagon.

FIRST: Do you think they'd take a fancy to me?

SECOND: I wouldn't back on it.

*The* FIRST OLD WOMAN *gazes out of the window.*

FIRST: You can see what goes on from this top table. (*pause*) It's better than going down to that place on the embankment, anyway.

SECOND: Yes, there's not too much noise.

FIRST: There's always a bit of noise.

SECOND: Yes, there's always a bit of life.

*Pause.*

FIRST: They'll be closing down soon to give it a scrub-round.

SECOND: There's a wind out.

*Pause.*

FIRST: I wouldn't mind staying.

SECOND: They won't let you.

FIRST: I know. (*pause*) Still, they only close hour and half, don't they? (*pause*) It's not long. (*pause*) You can go along, then come back.

SECOND: I'm going. I'm not coming back.

FIRST: When it's light I come back. Have my tea.

SECOND: I'm going. I'm going up to the Garden.

FIRST: I'm not going down there. (*pause*) I'm going up to Waterloo Bridge.

SECOND: You'll just about see the last two-nine-six come up over the river.

FIRST: I'll just catch a look at it. Time I get up there.

*Pause.*

It don't look like an all-night bus in daylight, do it?

# LAST TO GO

*A coffee stall, A* BARMAN *and an old* NEWSPAPER SELLER. *The* BARMAN *leans on his counter, the* OLD MAN *stands with tea.*

*Silence.*

MAN: You was a bit busier earlier.

BARMAN: Ah.

MAN: Round about ten.

BARMAN: Ten, was it?

MAN: About then.

*Pause.*

I passed by here about then.

BARMAN: Oh yes?

MAN: I noticed you were doing a bit of trade.

*Pause.*

BARMAN: Yes, trade was very brisk here about ten.

MAN: Yes, I noticed.

*Pause.*

MAN: I sold my last one about then. Yes. About nine forty-five.

BARMAN: Sold your last then, did you?

MAN: Yes, my last 'Evening News' it was. Went about twenty to ten.

*Pause.*

BARMAN: 'Evening News', was it?

MAN: Yes.

*Pause.*

Sometimes it's the 'Star' is the last to go.

BARMAN: Ah.

MAN: Or the ... whatsisname.

BARMAN: 'Standard'.

MAN: Yes.

*Pause.*

All I had left tonight was the 'Evening News'.

*Pause.*

BARMAN: Then that went, did it?

MAN: Yes.

*Pause.*

MAN: Like a shot.

*Pause.*

BARMAN: You didn't have any left, eh?

MAN: No. Not after I sold that one.

*Pause.*

BARMAN: It was after that you must have come by here then, was it?

MAN: Yes, I come by here after that, see, after I packed up.

BARMAN: You didn't stop here though, did you?

MAN: When?

BARMAN: I mean, you didn't stop here and have a cup of tea then, did you?

MAN: What, about ten?

BARMAN: Yes.

MAN: No, I went up to Victoria.

BARMAN: No, I thought I didn't see you.

MAN: I had to go up to Victoria.

*Pause.*

BARMAN: Yes, trade was very brisk here about then.

*Pause.*

MAN: I went to see if I could get hold of George.

204

BARMAN: Who?

MAN: George.

*Pause.*

BARMAN: George who?

MAN: George ... whatsisname.

BARMAN: Oh.

*Pause.*

Did you get hold of him?

MAN: No. No, I couldn't get hold of him. I couldn't locate him.

BARMAN: He's not about much now, is he?

*Pause.*

MAN: When did you last see him then?

BARMAN: Oh, I haven't seen him for years.

MAN: No, nor me.

*Pause.*

BARMAN: Used to suffer very bad from arthritis.

MAN: Arthritis?

BARMAN: Yes.

MAN: He never suffered from arthritis.

BARMAN: Suffered very bad.

*Pause.*

MAN: Not when I knew him.

*Pause.*

BARMAN: I think he must have left the area.

*Pause.*

MAN: Yes, it was the 'Evening News' was the last to go tonight.

BARMAN: Not always the last though, is it, though?

MAN: No. Oh no. I mean sometimes it's the 'News'. Other times it's one of the others. No way of telling beforehand. Until you've got your last one left, of course. Then you can tell which one it's going to be.

BARMAN: Yes.

*Pause.*

MAN: Oh yes.

*Pause.*

I think he must have left the area.

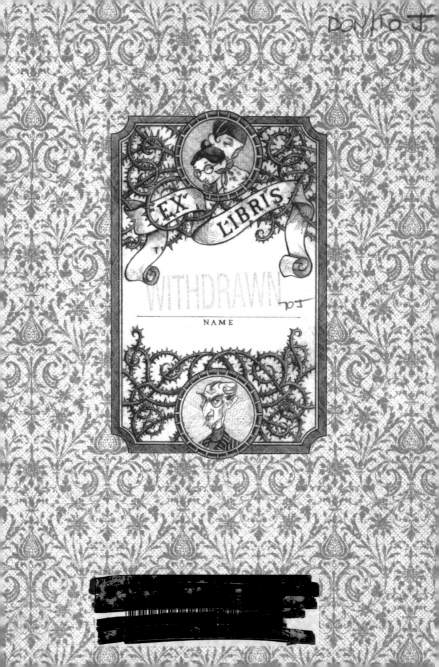

DON/TO J

EX LIBRIS

WITHDRAWN

NAME